SOVIET ARTS

STATE THEATRE, MUSIC AND CINEMA RESEARCH INSTITUTE

YURI SLONIMSKY

THE BOLSHOI BALLET NOTES

2nd REVISED AND ENLARGED EDITION

FOREIGN LANGUAGES PUBLISHING HOUSE

MOSCOW

ЮРИЙ СЛОНИМСКИЙ

БАЛЕТ БОЛЬШОГО ТЕАТРА

Заметки

TRANSLATED FROM THE RUSSIAN

DESIGNED BY *Y. KOPYLOV*

TEXT FOR FLAP AND BIBLIOGRAPHY
BY *N. ROSLAVLEVA*

MOST OF THE PHOTOGRAPHS ARE BY
Y. UMNOV.

OTHERS ARE BY *A. VOROTYNSKY*
AND *A. SAKHAROV,*

AND SOME FROM THE BAKHRUSHIN
THEATRICAL MUSEUM
OF MOSCOW.

FOREWORD TO THE SECOND EDITION

This new edition of my work, published a few years ago in connection with the Bolshoi Ballet's visit to London, is not a textually exact replica of the former one. The intervening years have introduced much that is new into the biography of the Bolshoi Theatre ballet: guest performances abroad, a considerably expanded repertoire and many talented young dancers.

All this obliged the author to revise the first edition, rewriting the main chapter "The Ballet Repertoire", enlarging some other chapters by adding information about young dancers at present holding prominent positions in the company, and replacing the old chapter "By Way of an Epilogue" with a new one—"Our Points of View", wherein, albeit briefly, are posed the aesthetic precepts of Soviet ballet.

Limitations of space prevent me from giving more exhaustive appraisals of dancers, choreographers and productions, or quote any foreign reviews.

I shall be most happy if I have succeeded in even partly improving my work in its second edition and thus assisting my readers in acquiring a true idea of the Bolshoi Ballet.

Yuri Slonimsky

February-March 1960
Leningrad

FROM THE AUTHOR

These notes are the impressions of a man who has for a long time followed the life and development of Soviet ballet. It goes without saying that I have tried to be as objective as possible. But my personal inclinations and experience as author of many ballet books could not fail to influence my appraisals, of course.

The volume of this pamphlet does not allow me to describe all that is interesting in the life of the Bolshoi Theatre. Our task is somewhat facilitated by the existence of British literature on Soviet ballet. I have in mind two books by the late Iris Morley, articles by Joan Lawson and other critics, Bogdanov-Berezovsky's book on Ulanova with a preface by Cyril Beaumont, Beaumont's comments on books of Soviet ballets in his capital work *The Complete Book of Ballets*, his monographs *The Ballet Called Swan Lake* and *The Ballet Called Giselle*, Evan Senior's book on Soviet music and theatre, Mary Clarke's articles in *The Dancing Times*, and so forth. We could challenge some of the opinions expressed in these works and question the accuracy of certain data, but we are gratified by the eagerness, with which the authors strove to arrive at an understanding of the complex processes going on in Soviet ballet, and the sincerity of their desire to understand our searchings and aims. We hope that mutual interest will continue to grow, for close contact holds out bright promise for the flourishing of ballet—an art which speaks the eloquent language of a warm heart and noble soul longing for peace and happiness.

May-June 1956

PAGES FROM THE HISTORY OF THE BOLSHOI THEATRE

In 1773 the Trusteeship Council of the Moscow Orphanage decided to start a ballet class* for its inmates. Muscovites were already familiar with ballet, and the Opera and Ballet Theatre was preparing to open its doors.**

Filippo Beccari, an Italian dancer, formerly of the St. Petersburg Court Theatre, offered his services as dancing master. The Trusteeship Council, however, was sceptical of his promise to turn the little orphans into expert dancers. To show the officials that he could do it, Beccari was willing to wait for his salary until his pupils became professional dancers, asking to be paid at the end of a three-year course 250 rubles for each solo dancer and 150 for those "who will be capable of performing a *'figure'* with perfect precision and will also acquit themselves well in *ballets pantomime*".

There were many who wanted to learn dancing. The pupils understood from the start that developing a talent meant hard work above all. "The children will jump without taking a rest for four hours on end, even to the detriment of their health"—reported the masters. And the result surpassed all expectations: of 62 pupils 24 became soloists.

Beccari was succeeded in 1778 by Leopold Paradis, who had once worked with the celebrated Hilferding. He undertook to train 30 children three times a week for three hours "in characters of *serio, comique* and *demi-comique*". He created a number of ballets on the private stage of the Orphanage and trained a second group of dancers. The lesser part of these became soloists of the St. Petersburg Court Theatre, the greater formed in 1780 the nucleus of the Petrovsky Theatre company.

The Petrovsky Theatre was located on that very spot where the Bolshoi Theatre now stands. It was opened with *Magic School*, a ballet by Paradis. The key roles were danced almost exclusively by Moscow Orphanage inmates, among them Mavra Poliskova, Matryona Andreyeva, Yegor Tyomin, and Matvei Bakin. The company numbered at that time twenty-one dancers.

The Orphanage thus became the cradle of ballet training in Moscow, and its school—the backbone of a permanent Moscow ballet theatre.

* Earlier—from 1766 children were taught ballroom dancing in the class of Pyotr Maximov, dancing master of Moscow University.

** The genealogy of the Bolshoi Theatre dates from 1776, when ballets began to be staged regularly.

7

The Moscow theatre thrived because at the beginning it was free from Court tutelage, it catered for audiences that were more democratic than those in the capital and employed many actors from among former serfs. Another important factor was the popularity of various fairs and festivals among the Muscovites. The Moscow theatre had its distinctive features, reflected in its original repertoire and the specific features of its performance.

It was here, at the turn of the 19th century, that a new genre came into being—one inspired by the national comic opera—dance scenes suggested by folk festivals, games, Yule-tide and Shrove-tide carnivals, etc. These dances were created by Vasily Balashov, a former inmate of the Orphanage, soloist of the Court Stage at St. Petersburg and choreographer of the Petrovsky Theatre in Moscow. In his intermezzi the role of the hero—a plucky Russian lad who emerges with flying colours from any scrape—was invariably played by another former inmate of the Orphanage, the *buffo* Gavrila Ivanov-Raikov. Petersburg choreographers Ivan Valberg, A. Auguste and others after them borrowed and developed Balashov's methods. And in 1812-14 Russian folk dances were successfully shown by Charles Didelot and his colleagues in a Russian *divertissement* at King's Theatre, London.

From 1812 the Moscow ballet company was headed by Adam Gluszkowski—favourite pupil of Didelot, prominent Russian dancer, teacher and choreographer. His wife Tatyana was a wonderful ballerina whose praise was sung by poets.

Adam Gluszkowski was the first to draw on Pushkin's poems for ideas. He adapted for ballet *Ruslan and Lyudmila*—one of the poet's earliest works (1821). Its great popularity in Moscow enabled it to be presented in St. Petersburg three years later. In 1827 Gluszkowski staged his second Pushkin ballet—*The Prisoner in the Caucasus* (the libretto was written in 1823 in St. Petersburg by Didelot to music by Cavos). Contemporaries have left eulogies about the memorable performances by the beautiful Tatyana Gluszkowska as the gay and faithful Lyudmila and the passionate and courageous Circassian girl.

For many years the Moscow ballet did not have a good stage to perform on. The Petrovsky Theatre was destroyed by fire in 1805, while the Arbat Theatre, built in 1808, burned down during the Patriotic War in 1812. While the present Bolshoi Theatre was under construction, the ballet company which was quite small (only 38 dancers in 1811), had to dance on makeshift stages. When the Bolshoi Theatre was opened in 1825 the company numbered 47 dancers.

The 1820s and 1830s were eventful years at the Bolshoi. Its audiences were the first to hear the sparkling merry music of Alabyev (*The Magic Drum*, 1828) and Varlamov (*Diversions of the Sultan*, 1834, and *Tom Thumb*, 1837). Here, in 1828, they saw *Othello* as a ballet, created by the famous Italian choreographer Vigano, and mounted in Moscow by Fortunato Bernardelli. The latter staged here his *Richard Coeur de Lion in Palestine* (1829) after Walter Scott's novel *The Talisman*. Félicité Hullin* (Sor by marriage) created a heroic ballet *Fenella*, based on Auber's opera of the same title, which had been banned by the Russian censors.

In 1837, St. Petersburg ballet-goers witnessed the Russian *début* of Maria Taglioni. At the same time ballet lovers in Moscow were introduced to Yekaterina Sankovskaya, justly named the Russian Taglioni. Belinsky and Herzen called her the favourite of Moscow students, while the writer Saltykov-Shchedrin said she was a herald of truth, beauty and goodness. These words

---

* A good dancer and an excellent teacher she trained many gifted Moscow dancers. Her productions at the Bolshoi were distinguished by their progressive spirit. Hullin became a Russian subject and changed her Christian name for the Russian Felitsata.

described one of the major principles of Russian aesthetic approach to the classical dance: a ballet hero is beautiful only when reflecting the beauty of thought, feeling and deed. Sankovskaya personified spiritual purity and moral strength, and the Moscow audiences loved her for these qualities.

Chance willed it that in her old age she should become the first dancing teacher of the famous Stanislavsky.

Saltykov-Shchedrin said that Sankovskaya was more than a ballerina, she was a plastic interpreter of a new word. On the Russian stage this new word was romanticism, which reached its peak in the 1830s. Deeper interest in man's inner life—in his psychology and emotions—and especially in the lyrical sphere of feelings called for a reform in art. The genre "scènes de la vie privée", mythological tableaux and classical tragedies prevalent in the repertoire heretofore, now gave way to romantic legends and fairy-tales dealing chiefly with the dramatic vicissitudes of woman's destiny. This new, primarily lyrical content gave rise to an impetuous development of corresponding means of expression, especially in the case of danseuses. The technique of dancing sur les pointes, jumps and leaps imitating the state of flight, soaring poses en arabesque and attitude, alongside with terre à terre steps existing previously, enabled the choreographers to truthfully convey the feelings of their romantic heroes and heroines. Pantomime ballets, in which the dance served only as a link between mimed scenes, gave way to dance suites. Mime was reduced to the role of connecting tissue in these. Dance as means of moulding an image became the main thing. The way to romantic reform in the dance was paved by Didelot's Flore et Zéphyre.

The first triumphant tours of Russian ballerinas in Western Europe took place in the forties. The Muscovite Nadezhda Bogdanova*, who later became ballerina of the Bolshoi Theatre, was applauded in Paris, Berlin, Vienna and Milan. And Zina Richard, who was the granddaughter of Sergei Lopukhin, soloist of the Petrovsky theatre and adopted son of Paradis, became first a dancer and then teacher at the Paris Opéra.

The Russian romantic ballet, beginning with the times of Didelot, introduced a new hero into the system of ballet imagery—the people. Herefrom followed the rapid growth of ensemble in ballet. In 1850 the ballet company of the Bolshoi already numbered 155 dancers, 118 of whom comprised the corps de ballet, huge for the times.

The 1860s saw the commencement of a new stage in the development of Russian art. The movement for emancipation was breathing new life into all its spheres, ballet included.

It was then that Vasily Geltser, the dancer, mime and teacher, father of the famous Yekaterina Geltser, began his glorious career. At the Bolshoi there emerged a splendid danseur noble and original choreographer in the person of Sergei Sokolov, who was highly spoken of by Carlo Blasis. Sokolov's creations (especially the ballet Fern, staged in 1867), gave food for thought not only to choreographers but to musicians as well, among them the young Tchaikovsky.

In 1861-64 the great choreographer and teacher Carlo Blasis worked at the Bolshoi Theatre and its school. His Moscow pupils, becoming teachers in turn, have preserved to our days some special features of the Blasis school.

The wistfully lovely melodies of Tchaikovsky's Swan Lake were first heard in the Bolshoi Theatre on February 20, 1877 (O.S.). Conservative critics failed to understand his music and claimed it

---

* Foreign tours of the famed Yelena Andreyanova, Tatyana Smirnova and other Petersburg ballerinas are not mentioned in this story.

was . . . poor in melody. Julius Reisinger, responsible for the first choreography of *Swan Lake*, was unable to translate the score into proper scenic vision. Another balletmaster, Joseph Hansen, tried hard to breathe life into the ballet, but he failed too. It was only some twenty years later that Lev Ivanov created through the dance a lyrical image of the swan and made *Swan Lake* the brilliant success it has been ever since.

Tchaikovsky achieved what the best of his predecessors had striven for. He made ballet, in terms of ideas and characters, a legitimate branch of the musical theatre. Music became the most faithful servant of the dance and at the same time its real master. It could now be "plastically felt" and "visionally heard", irrespective of whether one was seeing the ballet or just listening to the music.

The enchanting music of *Swan Lake* and its poetic and inspired images were expressive of noble feelings which, in their turn, gave spiritual beauty to the classical dance. Tchaikovsky "humanised" ballet, opening new vistas before it. The stage dance was entering a new era.

The 1890s were the years of ballet's florescence. In the last decade of the 19th century Russian theatres staged three ballets by Tchaikovsky, three by Glasunov, Borodin's *Polovtsian Dances* (shown for the first time), and Drigo's *Les Millions d'Arlequin*. Arensky composed his *Egyptian Nights* in the same period, while dance compositions were created to the music of Glinka's *Waltz Fantasy*, Liszt's *Second Rhapsody* and Chopin's piano pieces.

It was in these years that Petipa and Ivanov attained the heights of mastery in their art; Alexander Gorsky was starting activity as choreographer and Mikhail Fokine, later an outstanding choreographer, was first attracting attention as a gifted dancer. And it was in these same years that the Russian school produced a galaxy of remarkable ballerinas, headed by Anna Pavlova. Several serious books on ballet, penned by Russian authors, appeared in that period. The syllabuses of ballet education were completely revised and new ones elaborated. Vladimir Stepanov worked out a remarkable system of dance notation which later enabled theatres the world over to re-create ballets, produced in Russia.

The turn of the century marked a new phase in the history of Moscow ballet. It was influenced by a number of factors, such as the opening of the Mamontov Opera House—the theatre which gave the world Fyodor Chaliapin and where the painters Serov, Vrubel, Vasnetsov, Golovin, Korovin and Polenov started their careers as scenic designers, and the founding of the Art Theatre by Stanislavsky and Nemirovich-Danchenko. The prevailing atmosphere of ardent seekings and struggle against routine and mediocrity shaped the artistic world outlook of Gorsky, then a young choreographer and teacher.

A pupil of Petipa, who had been given prominent roles in the first performances of Tchaikovsky's and Glasunov's ballets, Gorsky started with creating a class of improvisation at the St. Petersburg ballet school, a class where future ballerinas, among them Karsavina and Vaganova, learned to interpret classical music of Schumann and Liszt, Glinka and Chopin through the dance.

In 1899-1900 he revived for the Bolshoi Theatre *The Sleeping Beauty*, *Raymonda* and *Swan Lake* and then produced totally revised versions of old ballets, offering, in effect, new artistic approaches. The Bolshoi ballet repertoire was replenished with new productions, wherein Gorsky implemented his artistic principles, which were to become the basis of the entire ensuing practice of the Moscow ballet. To such productions, which vividly reveal Gorsky's tendencies as a daring innovator, belong *Don Quixote*, *The Little Humpbacked Horse* and *Le Corsaire*.

For many years Gorsky had been cherishing the idea of staging Flaubert's *Salammbô*. He finally did so in 1910 to music by Andrei Arends, with scenery and costumes designed by Konstantin Korovin. With this ballet and with *Gudula's Daughter* (after Hugo), staged somewhat earlier, he continued the traditional co-operation between the ballet theatre and classical literature, making full use of choreography to depict the characters and the essence of the dramatic conflict of the novel. *Salammbô* was followed by *Love Is Fast*, imbued with the spirit of folk life. The story was after La Motté-Fouque's *Undine*, the music—selected from Grieg's compositions. *Schubertiana* was done to Franz Schubert's pieces. In 1915 Gorsky made the first experimental translation of a symphony—that of Glasunov's Fifth—into dance idiom.

All his life Gorsky fought against the elements of dress concert in which ballet then abounded. He wanted the dancers to live their parts, for he could not envision a ballet image without character. Consequently he demanded the expressive means of ballet to be developed to the utmost. In his productions Gorsky departed from conventional pattern. Every ballet should have its own expressive idiom, he taught. Everything should be subordinated to the creation of an image. His dances were packed with detail, which lent them the necessary *local colour* whether in the form of folk dance elements or simple gestures.

Carried away by his seekings, Gorsky sometimes went to extremes. Speaking of the early days of his own career, Stanislavsky said: "My search for new ways was rather disorderly. I would dash from one extreme to another, taking along what I had found earlier." This could well apply to Gorsky. He keenly felt that it was no longer possible to create in the old way and this feeling determined his whole activity. "Art that does not create anything is doomed to death, to self-destruction," he would say. "You must create."

Gorsky's creative quest rallied the best dancers of the Bolshoi. Among those who took part in his productions were remarkable ballerinas such as Lyubov Roslavleva, Yekaterina Geltser and Adelina Giuri, all of whom started their careers in the 1890s. Roslavleva, an outstanding lyrical dancer, died very early and Giuri soon retired from the stage. The whole burden of the repertoire fell to Yekaterina Geltser and for thirty years she maintained the fame of Moscow ballet. Having started with a brilliant success in *Raymonda*, she finished her glorious career with *Red Poppy*, the first Soviet ballet.

Yekaterina Geltser was first taught by her father and then by Christian Johansson, Lev Ivanov and Vasily Tikhomirov. Her dancing virtuosity, particularly in *terre à terre* technique, was combined with great expressiveness and deep meaning. Broad and sweeping gestures, expressive mime and temperamental strong movement were characteristic of her manner. Moreover, besides being a gifted ballerina she was also an active figure in Russian theatre, and most of the progressive searchings of the Moscow ballet were directly connected with her creative endeavour.

Vasily Tikhomirov, an outstanding dancer, actor and teacher, a pupil of the celebrated Johansson, worked side by side with Gorsky despite the fact that they disagreed on some points. Tikhomirov amazed his contemporaries with his exceptional gifts. Beautifully built, manly and powerful, possessing an absolute purity of execution, he combined these qualities with a sweeping breadth of mime and sculptured perfection of movement. Tikhomirov became keeper and propagandist of the classical heritage in the Moscow ballet. As a teacher he trained more than one generation of ballet dancers, and many of those who built up the glory of the Moscow company both in pre- and post-revolutionary years owe their professional skill to him.

Gorsky's ballets often featured Mikhail Mordkin, a wonderful dancer, at home in whatever role he had to dance or act. He gave memorable performances as Mathô in *Salammbô*, as the charming and genial Basil in *Don Quixote*, the wistful Prince in *Swan Lake* and the happy-go-lucky fisherman in *Love Is Fast*.

The lively, emotional expressiveness of Mordkin and the sculptured majesty of Tikhomirov typified the Moscow school of classical dance. The movements of the Bolshoi dancers were imbued with strength, temperament and willpower. Moscow ballerinas, with Geltser first and foremost, captivated their audiences by their speed and expressiveness, combined with eloquent mime. This style of execution was later adopted most happily by young dancers of Moscow and Leningrad.

Together with the Petersburg ballet companies, Moscow dancers made many a triumphant tour abroad, taking part in the *Ballet Russe* seasons, organised by Serge Diaghilev, beginning with 1909.

The names of Sophia Fyodorova, Vera Karalli, Victorina Krieger, Maria Reisen, Yelena Adamovich, Margarita Kandaurova, Lavrenty Novikov, Alexander Volinin, Fyodor Kozlov, Leonid Zhukov, Leonide Massine, Vyacheslav Svoboda, Vladimir Ryabtsev and Ivan Sidorov—pupils of Tikhomirov, Gorsky and other famous teachers of the day—were well known abroad.

In the last pre-revolutionary years, however, there was a decline in Russian ballet. New productions became much rarer. Gorsky and Fokine were repeating their old experiments more and more often. Many dancers left the imperial theatres to tour the country or work for the films.

The Moscow Ballet School admitted no new pupils between 1906 and 1910. It resumed admission in 1911-12, but on a much smaller scale. In 1915 it was again stopped. This was part of the general crisis that spread to all spheres of art on the eve of the First World War.

A new phase in the life of the Bolshoi Ballet began after the Great October Socialist Revolution. Even in the early period of Soviet power, though exhausted by four years of the world war and three of the civil, the country managed to set aside part of its meagre budget to keep the theatres going. The government showed particular concern for the country's oldest theatres—the Bolshoi, Maly and Art theatres in Moscow and the Mariinsky, Mikhailovsky and Alexandrinsky theatres in Leningrad. Their doors were thrown open to hundreds of thousands of new theatre-goers—workers, peasants and soldiers. Close and warm-hearted contact was established between the theatre and the audiences.

The Moscow Ballet School resumed activity in 1920 on a new, broader basis of special and academic subjects.

Most of the Moscow ballet veterans remained at their posts. Gorsky headed the ballet company of the Bolshoi right to his death in 1924, while Arends, one of the country's oldest conductors and ballet composers, was in charge of its orchestra. He was succeeded by Yuri Fayer, who has been conducting ballets at the Bolshoi for over 45 years in the course of which he became one of the greatest living authorities on this special branch of conductor's art.

Moscow ballet lovers gratefully remember the coquettish and faminine Anastasya Abramova, the lyrically delicate Valentina Kudryavtseva, the excellent classical dancer Nina Podgoretskaya, the pathetic Lyubov Bank and the majestically beautiful Yelena Ilyushchenko. We remember Victor Smoltsov, excellent *danseur noble* in the first years after the Revolution, as Siegfried and Basil. His colleague Nikolai Tarasov, an outstanding teacher at the Moscow Ballet School, has trained many dancers now well known for their performance of Siegfried, Romeo, Désiré or Albrecht.

In the early 1920s the Bolshoi company was joined by Asaf Messerer, Igor Moiseyev and Mikhail Gabovich, all of whom later became prominent figures in Soviet ballet.

Messerer—a dancer of outstanding talent and superb technique—performed any dance with brilliant ease, be it eccentric, grotesque, character or strictly academic. The ease with which he would rise into the air and the perfection of his classical line were amazing. His repertoire included not only leading classical roles, but a number of parts he himself had created and perfected—such masterpieces as the Fanatic in *Salammbô*, the Skater in *The Prisoner in the Caucasus* and the dance of the Chinese bronze statuette in *Red Poppy*. At present he acts as the Bolshoi company balletmaster, teaches at the School and produces ballets.

The name of Mikhail Gabovich has been linked for a quarter of a century with the evolvement of a new repertoire at the Bolshoi. As the leading *danseur noble*, Gabovich displayed a fine sense of the artistic and an ability to penetrate into the psychology of his characters. His many gifts enabled him to create such different roles, as Albrecht and Romeo, Yevgeny (*The Bronze Horseman*) and Andrei (*Taras Bulba*), the Prince in *Cinderella* and Ma Li-cheng in *Red Poppy*. Gabovich now teaches, writes ballet criticism and participates in forums.

Moiseyev began his career as a character dancer and was acclaimed as a very interesting artist. However, he soon switched on to choreography, creating at the Bolshoi *The Football-Player*, a new version of *Salammbô*, *Three Fat Men* and *Spartacus*. Moiseyev's contribution to the dance culture of the Soviet Union can hardly be overestimated.

A Folk Dance group was founded on his initiative in 1937 on a lavish scale. Thanks to Moiseyev, that subtle, clever and gifted connoisseur of folk dancing, dozens of long forgotten gems of folklore have been restored to life. Through performing dances of various peoples of the world Moiseyev and his company enriched our knowledge of folk dance. And not only ours. The whole world knows the Moiseyev company. The experience of the Moiseyev dance group has helped to establish many similar folk-dance companies in Soviet republics and abroad.

Soviet power gave all the art workers full freedom of critical assimilation of the old and of bold quest for the new. At first some masters of the ballet were inclined to reject the whole legacy of the pre-revolutionary ballet. Instead they offered experimental productions of all kinds. There was "neo-classical" and "abstract" ballet, which consisted of nothing but formal dance patterns, eurythmics and plastique, buffoonery turned into dance, mimed dramas, *tableaux vivants*, acrobatic *études* and "dances of machines in a modern city".

In the 1920s, Soviet ballet went through all the infectious phases of "natural" barefoot dancing, affected constructivism, broken lines of expressionism and erotic orientalism.

However, practice and time—these great exposers of all and every flitting delusion—revealed the truth. It appeared that all these formalistic innovations, conceived through the rejection of the classical heritage and its traditions in contemporary art, were short-lived and led nowhere, while the best of this classical heritage constituted a reliable foundation on which to build the new. It was also proved that the audiences preferred classical ballets to novel extravaganzas.

Classical ballet gained in popularity with every new season.

In 1919 the Bolshoi showed its first production of the *Nutcracker* in Gorsky's original interpretation. The following year he and Nemirovich-Danchenko staged an experimental production of *Swan Lake*. In 1922 some of this experience was used by Gorsky in a new version of the ballet. The Bolshoi also revived *The Sleeping Beauty*.

On the tenth anniversary of the October Revolution, the Bolshoi staged Glière's *Red Poppy*. The book of the ballet was written by Mikhail Kurilko, the designer of the settings. He worked in close contact with Geltser and Tikhomirov who performed the leads of a Chinese dancer and Soviet

1. Bolshoi Petrovsky Theatre (built in 1824)
2. Folk festivities in a village near Moscow (painting by an unknown artist, 19th century)
3. Adam Gluszkowski as Raoul in *Raoul de Créquis* by K. Didelot
4. Yekaterina Sankovskaya
5. Félicité Hullin-Sor as Cinderella
6. Irakly Nikitin, a dancer of the 1840s, as Colas in *La Fille Mal Gardée*

DANCERS OF THE LATE 19TH CENTURY

7. Praskovya Lebedeva
8. Marfa Muravyova
9. Olga Nikolayeva
10. Vasily Geltser
11. Scene from *Swan Lake* staged in Moscow in 1877

12. Lyubov Roslavleva as Aurora (*The Sleeping Beauty*)
13. Sergei Sokolov, Moscow dancer and ballet master, in *Don Quixote*
14. Alexander Gorsky as faun
15. Alexander Gorsky

16, 19. Anna Sobeshchanskaya and Pelageya Karpakova,
the first performers of Odette in *Swan Lake*
17. Scene from *Salammbô* staged in 1910 by A. Gorsky
18. Yekaterina Geltser and Mikhail Mordkin as
Salammbô and Mathô

20. Yekaterina Geltser as Tsar-Maiden (*The Little Hump-backed Horse*)
21. Yekaterina Geltser and Vasily Tikhomirov (*Dream Dance* staged by A. Gorsky)
22. Vasily Tikhomirov as Basil (*Don Quixote*)

23. Mikhail Mordkin as Pierrot (concert number)
24. Yekaterina Geltser as Tao Hoa (*Red Poppy*)
25. Mikhail Mordkin in "Bacchanalia" to A. Glazunov's music
26. Lavrenty Novikov in *Salammbô*
27. Mikhail Mordkin in *Don Quixote*

28

29

30

31

28. Sophia Fyodorova as Esmeralda (*Gudula's Daughter*)
29. Alexander Volinin in *The Sleeping Beauty*
30. Sophia Fyodorova and Lavrenty Novikov in "Bacchanalia"
31. Vladimir Ryabtsev as Marcelline (*La Fille Mal Gardée*)
32. Vera Karalli in Glazunov's Fifth Symphony staged by A. Gorsky
33. Ivan Sidorov as khan in *The Little Humpbacked Horse*
34. Margarita Kandaurova in "Butterfly" concert number (music by R. Drigo, choreography by A. Gorsky)

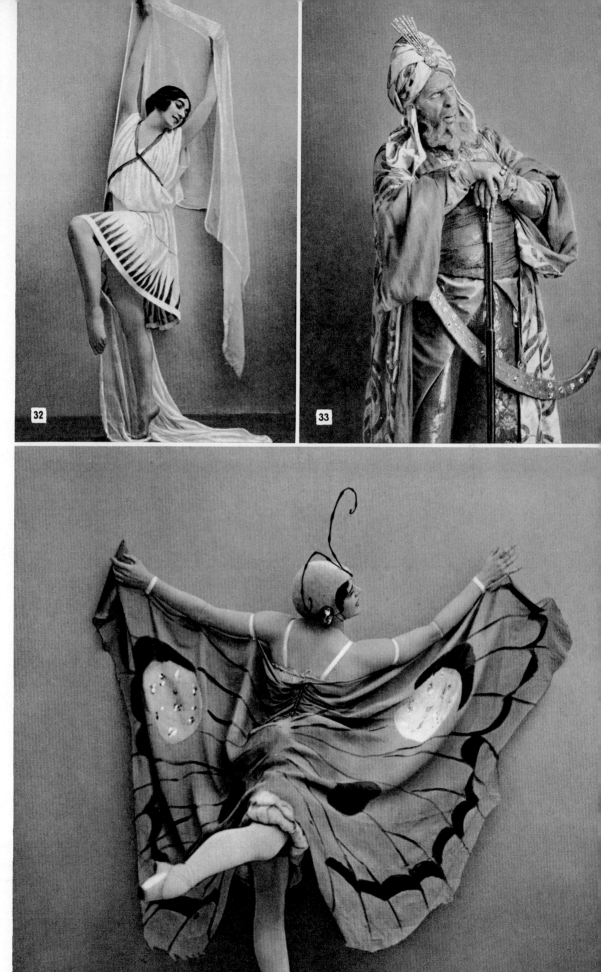

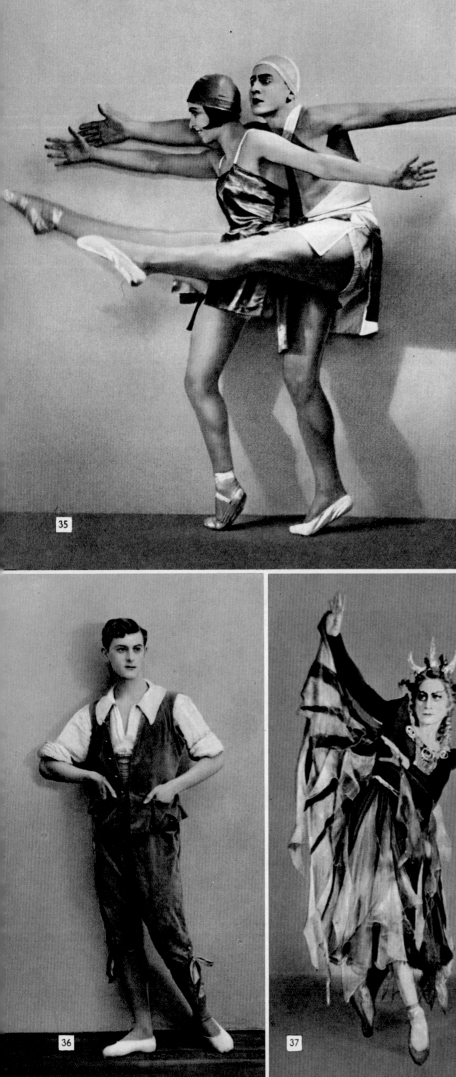

35. Anastasia Abramova and Mikhail Gabovich in a concert number (choreography by K. Goleizovsky)
36. Victor Smoltsov as Colas *(La Fille Mal Gardée)*
37. Victorina Kriger as Lilac Fairy in *The Sleeping Beauty*
38. Valentina Kudryavtseva as Nicea *(La Bayadère)*
39. Ballet master Kasyan Goleizovsky
40. Vera Karalli and Alexandra Balashova in *Giselle*
41. Lyubov Bunk in *Josef the Beautiful* (staged by K. Goleizovsky)

42. Alexei Bulgakov as Monster *(The Crimson Flower)*
43. Nina Podgoretskaya in "Walpurgis Night", ballet scene from the opera *Faust*
44. Mikhail Gabovich as faun *(Esmeralda)*

45. Marina Semyonova as Nicea *(La Bayadère)*
46. Marina Semyonova as Odette *(Swan Lake)*

47. Asaf Messerer as Chinese God (Red Poppy)
48. Asaf Messerer as fanatic (Salammbô, staged by I. Moiseyev)
49. Alexei Yermolayev in the dream scene in the ballet Red Flower
50. Mikhail Gabovich as Andrei (Taras Bulba)

49

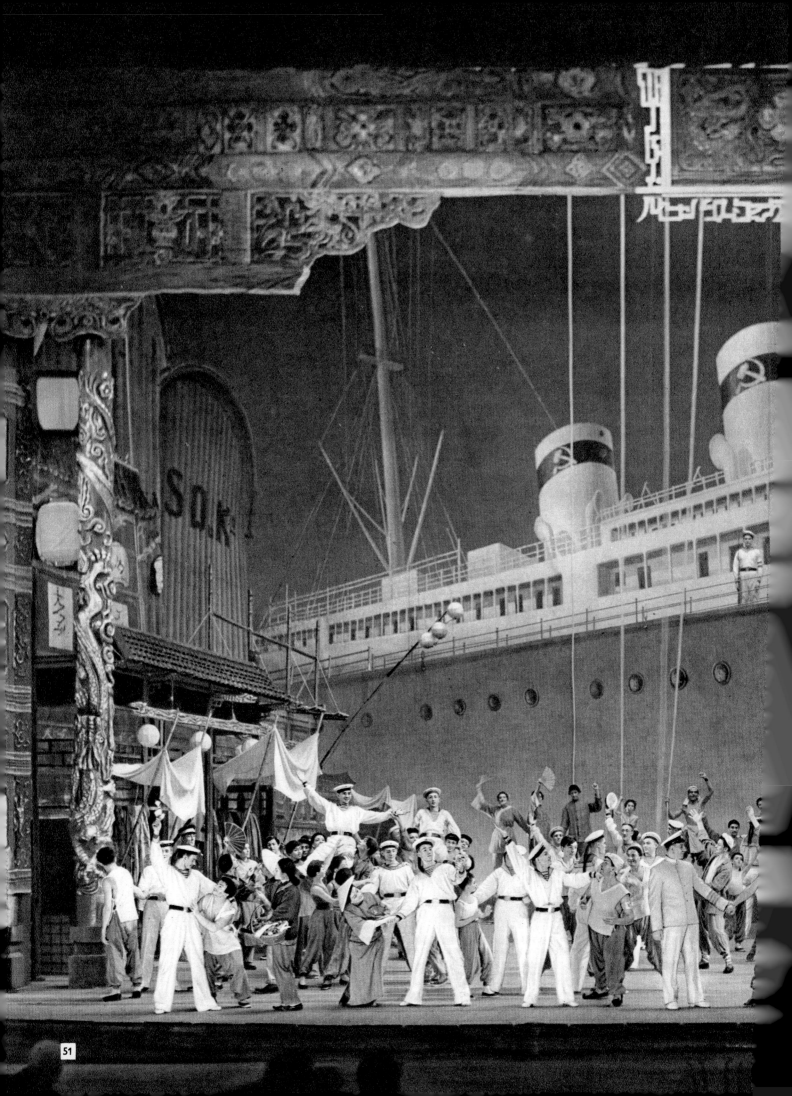

53

54

1. Scene from the ballet *Red Flower* (1949)
2. Alexei Yermolayev as Tybalt (*Romeo and Juliet*)
3. Sulamith Messerer in *Don Quixote*
4. Olga Lepeshinskaya and Asaf Messerer in *Nutcracker*

OLGA LEPESHINSKAYA
55. as Suok with Alexander Radunsky as
    Doctor Gaspar (Three Fat Men)
56. as Kitri (Don Quixote)
57. as Svetlana (Svetlana)
58. as Tao Hoa (Red Flower)

59

60

GALINA ULANOVA
59. with Mikhail Gabovich in
    Romeo and Juliet
60. in *Swan Lake*
61. in *Giselle*

captain, respectively. Another performer of the leading male role in the *Red Poppy* was Alexei Bulgakov, veteran mime of the ballet, colleague of Petipa, Gorsky and Fokine. The choreographers were Tikhomirov and Lev Lashchilin. The latter produced the most responsible scenes—those in the Chinese harbour.

There was much that was naïve in theme, music and production, and yet the *Red Poppy* scored an unparalleled success and was presented 200 times in two seasons. It was staged in practically every town of the Soviet Union and was the first truly popular Soviet ballet. Many of the dances became part of the repertoire of amateur dance groups. No concert could do without some number from the *Red Poppy*. Yekaterina Geltser often did the variations of Tao Hoa, the heroine, Asaf Messerer performed solos of the Bronze Statuette (a difficult dance abounding in high jumps) and the Ribbon Dance. "Yablochko"—Soviet sailors' dance to a popular folk melody, performed by talented young dancers of the Bolshoi, literally swept the country.

The *Red Poppy* is prominent in the history of Soviet ballet as the first successful attempt to render a contemporary theme, the theme of the national-liberation movement, on the ballet stage.

To play the lead in the musical and choreographic life of the country, the Bolshoi had to enlarge its ballet company, reinforce it with young talent and enlist the assistance of the best available teachers. That explains the transfer to Moscow, in the late twenties and the early thirties, of a group of Leningrad dancers, headed by the young Marina Semyonova and Alexei Yermolayev.

Graduates of the same school, they started their career almost at the same time (she made her *début* in 1925 and he a year later), and for a long time appeared together. Semyonova and Yermolayev became prominent exponents of the Soviet style of dancing. Seeking for new media in which to create their own individual dance imagery, they enriched the virtuosity of classical dancing which for both of them was the main and most eloquent idiom.

Critics stressed particularly the vivid national character of Semyonova's dancing. Watching her, one thought of Nekrasov's lines about Russian women:

> The gracious, calm and stately miens,
> The movements, full of graceful power,
> The eyes, the looks, the gait of queens.

Semyonova, like the women sung by the Russian poet, "seemed to shine as a sun-ray when she passed". She combined an expressive melodiousness of movement—a quality rare and most precious in a dancer—with a perfect execution of intricate steps, turns and leaps, and wonderful statuelike poses. Her dazzling dance, characterised by poise and strength, lent a festive air to every production in which she appeared. These gifts enabled her to give an original interpretation of the old ballets. She created a new Odette and Odile, and presented Nicea the bayadère in a new light—as a woman fighting for human dignity, for the right to love and be loved.

The choreographic portraits created by Alexei Yermolayev were coloured by his vibrant, powerful talent. Plasticity of line, expressiveness of movement, ability to make his gestures speak, and deep penetration into his characters, all went to make an event out of his every appearance on the stage. Although mainly a classical dancer, Yermolayev was also good in eccentric, grotesque and comedy roles, dancing the barber Basil, the Moor Abderrahman, the Marseille revolutionary Philippe, the saboteur Li Shang-fu, the merciless and vengeful Tybalt and the woman-hater Ripafratta.

Among the Leningrad teachers who were transferred to the Moscow Ballet School and theatre, were Yelizaveta Gerdt, who had inherited Johansson's teaching methods and was also a pupil of

62. Maya Plisetskaya *(Swan Lake)*

Fokine; Alexander Chekrygin, formerly an interesting character mime and dancer, Alexander Monakhov—a good character dancer, who became one of the founders of the syllabus for character dancing, and Victor Semyonov—an outstanding *danseur noble* of a strictly academic style.

This was the beginning of fruitful co-operation between the Leningrad and Moscow ballet schools and it led to the blending of various styles into one—a unified style with its own original features. The new graduates mastered the best achievements of Leningrad and Moscow ballet. Worthy of special mention among these newcomers is Olga Lepeshinskaya, who made her Bolshoi Theatre *début* in 1933.

An easy, spontaneous and vigorously exhilirating manner, a sense of humour and pronounced histrionic gifts, considerable extension, excellent *équilibre sur les pointes*, exceptional ability for performance of virtuosity steps (especially *pirouettes*)—such are Lepeshinskaya's gifts, which have gained her wide popularity. Her abilities as *comedienne* and her bravura virtuosity were fully revealed in the roles of Lise and Kitri in the old ballets *La Fille Mal Gardée* and *Don Quixote*, and in the parts of Swanilda and Fadette (in the Delibes ballets). She is particularly good in portraying contemporary heroines, and this feeling of contemporaneity has enabled her to maintain through all the ballets and recitals she has ever taken part in the image of a girl of our times—vivacious, merry, full of zest and initiative. Svetlana (in the ballet of the same name, to be discussed below) was an important milestone in the career of this talented artist.

More talent came to the Bolshoi. In 1936 the company was joined by Pyotr Gusev, a clever actor, an excellent teacher (particularly of supported adagio). Maria Kozhukhova, a first-class teacher and a former Mariinsky ballerina, also came to work at the Bolshoi school. There were more newcomers from Leningrad at practically the same time: *danseur noble* Vladimir Preobrazhensky, who became Lepeshinskaya's partner, Sergei Koren, the first Mercutio in Moscow, an excellent character dancer and populariser of Spanish dances, choreographers Vasily Vainonen and Rostislav Zakharov.

Soviet ballet made great strides in the thirties. New ballets, which have since become Soviet classics, were staged. Outstanding dancers, choreographers, musicians, book authors, critics and stage designers came to the fore. Ballet creations were enriched with new subjects, and new genres were developed; means of expression were extended and the importance of *theatre* as integral part of ballet directing considerably enhanced.

The Bolshoi repertoire was enlarged to include some excellent new productions: *The Flames of Paris* (music by Boris Asafiev, book by Nikolai Volkov and Vladimir Dmitriev, choreography by Vasily Vainonen), which tells of the heroism of the French revolutionaries of 1789, Pushkin's romantic poems *The Fountain of Bakhchisarai* and *The Prisoner in the Caucasus* (music by Asafiev, book by Volkov, choreography by Zakharov), Yuri Olesha's fairy-tale *Three Fat Men* (music by Oransky, book and choreography by Igor Moiseyev), Gogol's patriotic epic *Taras Bulba* (music by Solovyov-Sedoi, book by Kaplan, choreography by Zakharov).

There were only two ballets dealing with contemporary themes and but one of them, the *Red Poppy*, had real popularity. However, this ballet was largely dedicated to the heroic people of China. The honour of creating the first ballets about Soviet people belonged to the authors of *Baby Stork* and *Svetlana* (composer Dmitry Klebanov, choreographers Alexander Radunsky, Nikolai Popko and Lev Pospekhin). Their heroes are ordinary people: Soviet children in *Baby Stork*, and Komsomol builders of a new town in the Far East in *Svetlana*. They all live a life of lofty and noble interests. Soviet patriotism, which is the main theme in *Svetlana*, is closely linked with

the theme of fraternal solidarity of all honest labourers in the wide world, told through the medium of childishly naïve, but charming characters of *Baby Stork*. Children's audiences are invariably stirred by such scenes from *Baby Stork* as teaching the orphaned baby stork how to fly, rallying all animals and children to help the little Negro boy, and also by the friendship of all children of the U.S.S.R. and Africa. Small wonder that *Baby Stork* has already had a run of over twenty years. The new contemporary heroes won the love of large audiences. *Svetlana* has been produced by many theatres. The classical septet (game with a floating scarf), the dance of Stepan's enemy, pretending to be his friend, and the lyrical *pas de deux* have added to the treasury of Soviet ballet.

Roles from the classic heritage help the artists to perfect their dancing craft. But a dancer's personality can best be revealed in new roles made especially for him or her. That is why new ballets are so welcome, even though they sometimes lack the perfection of the greatest classics.

New ballets brought new talents to the fore. Yermolayev scored a great success as Philippe in *The Flames of Paris* and Tibul in *Three Fat Men*; Gabovich as Waclaw in *The Fountain of Bakhchisarai*, the Prisoner in *The Prisoner in the Caucasus* and Andrei in *Taras Bulba*; Lepeshinskaya as Suok in *Three Fat Men* and Svetlana in the ballet of that name; Yuri Kondratov revealed his gift as Ilko, the hero of *Svetlana*. Georgi Farmanyants gained wide popularity in the bouncing part of the Zaporozhye Cossack in *Taras Bulba*. Vera Vasilyeva became the first Maria (*The Fountain of Bakhchisarai*) in Moscow. The new ballets also produced such excellent character dancers as Nadezhda Kapustina, Valentina Galetskaya and Yadviga Sangovich. Particular mention should be made of Alexander Radunsky, an actor of great talent, one who knows how to create life-like character mime parts.

By 1940 the Bolshoi ballet company was 200 strong and included, apart from those mentioned above, many other talented ballerinas and *danseurs*, among them Sophia Golovkina, Sulamith Messerer, Irina Tikhomirnova, Marianna Bogolyubskaya, Nina Chorokhova (Chkalova), Yelena Chikvaidze, Alexander Rudenko, Alexei Zhukov, Anatoly Kuznetsov, Victor Tsaplin, Vladimir Golubin and many others.

The years of the Great Patriotic War, when the nazi hordes invaded the country and were advancing to Moscow, Leningrad and the Volga, were years of severe trial for art. Soviet art belied the saying: "When the cannon roar, the muses are silent." True, there were fewer *premières*, but the ballet company worked with redoubled effort. The Bolshoi was evacuated to Kuibyshev, where it remained for three years, producing there the new ballet *Crimson Sails* (music by Yurovsky, book after Grin, choreographers Radunsky, Popko and Pospekhin). A small group of dancers remained in Moscow where it performed at the Bolshoi Filial.

In 1940, the Bolshoi and its Filial presented 112 ballet performances. In 1942 the Bolshoi Filial alone gave 126 ballet performances and the main company in Kuibyshev gave another 89. The creative strength of the Bolshoi ballet was not diminished, but rather multiplied in these years of grave ordeal considering that teams toured the front lines performing for the troops, many dancers and personnel joined the Armed Forces and others left for work in dance ensembles.

The post-war years at the Bolshoi were quite eventful, but one event is particularly noteworthy: Galina Ulanova, who had often appeared as guest artist on the stage of the Bolshoi, now came to stay with the company. A successor of the best ballerinas of the past, Ulanova has become the unexcelled lyrical and tragic *danseuse* of our day. Her ability to express the most complex emotions naturally and simply, to make each movement and pose inspired and understandable, such are

64. Nina Timofeyeva (*Swan Lake*

some of her most captivating gifts. Ulanova does not go in for *bravura* dancing as such, she dances everything as if it is "whispered", with no intention of showing off. She does not act, she actually lives the dance.

The simplest thing in art is the most difficult, and that has been proved by Ulanova. Having achieved the heights of technical perfection, she knows how to conceal strain under an appearance of harmonious calm. She subordinates everything to one task—breathing life and thought into those steps which often seem superfluous and pointless. "Laconism", which has become Ulanova's motto, is also one of the precepts of the Russian school—it was Anna Pavlova's motto too.

Stanislavsky left us a wise definition of two types of ballerinas—representatives of two types of dance. Some ballerinas, he said, perform without being in the least concerned with the subject of the dance. For them the dance is a sequence of steps. They create form devoid of content and reproduce nothing but the external action in motion. Stanislavsky was highly critical of such ballerinas. They cannot, he stressed, achieve the main goal—make the invisible creative life visible.

But there are ballerinas of another type. They cultivate plasticity until it becomes part of them, their second nature. "These ballerinas," Stanislavsky wrote, "do not dance or act, they live the part."

We do not know whom Stanislavsky had in mind when he was writing these lines—Pavlova, Roslavleva, Geltser or someone else. But it fits Ulanova perfectly, just as if he was writing about her.

A ballet character is above all a dance character—an "inspired acting of the entire body" as Noverre defined it. Stanislavsky, who said as much, held that the main thing in a dance is its "melody", its cantilena, i.e., a flowing plastic line of movement. The dance "melody" requires harmonious movement of all parts of the body, to the very finger-tips. And harmony gives birth to truthful art.

The visible "music" of Ulanova's dance appeals to millions because through it she asserts the theme of noble love and heroic deeds, upholding her convictions as she sings them with her body.

In Ulanova's interpretation, the ordinary feelings of joy and grief, dreams of happiness and disillusion, resolution and hesitation, become extraordinary, or rather extraordinarily beautiful. Like with the girl in the well-known fairy-tale the tears she sheds turn into pearls. The old *Giselle*, returning to the repertoire of the Bolshoi Theatre for Ulanova, was illumined with the light of an entirely new reading. Ulanova's heroines are faithful not only to their hearts but also to their convictions. And that is something new. With her the art of dancing is not just poetry of a passionate heart—the best ballerinas of the past possessed this gift—but poetry of inspired thoughts as well.

Several ballets, created by Soviet choreographers, are connected with Ulanova's name. *Romeo and Juliet* first shown at the Kirov Theatre in Leningrad in 1940, is the unchallenged best. Leonid Lavrovsky, one of the most prominent Soviet choreographers, who came to the Bolshoi Theatre almost simultaneously with Ulanova, produced this ballet at the Bolshoi in 1946.

The names of many dancers of the senior generation are associated with new productions. But, alas, the years of dancing fame are lamentably short. At the Bolshoi we no longer see Marina Semyonova, Messerer, Yermolayev, Gabovich, or many other brilliant dancers. Some are engaged in producing ballets, others in teaching, and still others have gone into administration.

There are new ballerinas and *danseurs* ready to take over the legacy of previous generations. Among these are two pupils of Yelizaveta Gerdt—Maya Plisetskaya and Raisa Struchkova.

65. Marina Kondratyeva (*Giselle*)

Abroad, Plisetskaya is often called Ulanova's successor. This is erroneous. The most mature and original ballerina of the Bolshoi after Ulanova, Plisetskaya can by no means be called her substitute or her successor. She has her own genre and style of execution, in many respects the very opposite of Ulanova's.

One is immediately struck by Maya Plisetskaya's natural gifts: her proudly arched back, her strong, eloquent arms and hands, her turns and soaring leaps that are almost masculine in gusto. The broadness of her leaps is such that even the huge stage of the Bolshoi seems too small for her. Plisetskaya's dancing is impetuous, exciting and brilliant. The plastique of her dance is mostly of a dynamic nature, which sets her apart from most of the other ballerinas. Predominantly sharp, even rather eccentric line of the ballerina's movements is overwhelmingly expressive. Her individuality finds expression in unusual patterns; often, Plisetskaya departs from the traditional dance forms and thus lends her inimitable style to all her roles. However that which, if attempted by anyone else, would be considered entirely unorthodox, in the case of Plisetskaya seems desirable and, sometimes, the only possible interpretation. At the same time in such roles as Odette-Odile or the Dying Swan Plisetskaya's dancing acquires amazing fluidity and inspired lyricism.

Odette-Odile, Zarema, Laurencia, Kitri, Raymonda—the list of these roles alone speaks of Plisetskaya's many-faceted gifts.

Her best and latest role is that of the Mistress of the Copper Mountain in *The Tale of the Stone Flower*. There is much in this role that answers Plisetskaya's abilities and requirements. Like a slippery lizard, cunning and powerful, she artfully twines herself around Danila. She uses every step as a piercing spear in her merciless and wrathful combat with Severyan —the enemy of the heroes. Dominating yet submissive, she is both regally strong and weak like all creatures of her sex.

Raisa Struchkova is the exact opposite of Maya Plisetskaya in type of talent and range of artistic interests. With Plisetskaya virtuosity and *bravura* are the main if not the sole means of creating a character. With Struchkova, on the other hand, mime, gesture and poses are musts in a character. Her dancing is essentially graceful, elegant and simple. Some prefer Struchkova in comedy, others in lyrical and yet others in dramatic roles. However, all agree that her images are attractively feminine, that her best characters breathe the charm of youth, of *joi de vivre*. Her repertoire includes Giselle and Cinderella, Maria and Juliet. It is a great pity that the available ballets of the Bolshoi have not given Struchkova the chance to develop that facet of her talent which was particularly promising, namely, the lyrical comedy. Her scintillating Mirandolina the Innkeeper in the ballet rendering of Goldoni's well-known play was a revelation for the audiences. The roles of Lise in *La Fille Mal Gardée* and other heroines in comedy ballets of the Soviet repertoire still await Struchkova, holding in store much joy both for the actress and the audiences.

Nina Timofeyeva came to the Bolshoi Theatre from Leningrad, where she danced at the Kirov Theatre. One admires her Odile particularly. With her perfect virtuosity technique, Timofeyeva has created her own version of the Magician's daughter: while enticing the Prince she falls in love with him herself. Timofeyeva always thinks first and foremost of dance imagery when creating her characters, and this enables her to dance with success some roles from the repertoire of Plisetskaya. The young dancer is very good-looking: her small proud head is poised on a beautiful body, and her eyes are big and eloquent. The time has come for her to have *her own* roles, in which she could fully reveal her personality.

66. Rimma Karelskaya *(Swan Lake)*

While Nina Timofeyeva is a dancer of predominantly dramatic gifts, Marina Kondratyeva has a leaning for lyricism in dancing, but it is no more than a leaning, however. Having excellently mastered the roles of Bird-girl in *Shuraleh* and of Cinderella, she worked at three roles simultaneously in the course of one year. Giselle, Juliet and Katerina (*The Tale of the Stone Flower*)—such is her remarkable range. Completely at home with all the intricacies of classical technique, which is a ballet dancer's natural medium of expression, Marina Kondratyeva is touchingly natural and earnest in her plastic revelations, her jump is ethereally light. Our story leaves her en route to maturity, which promises to bring out new facets of the ballerina's talent.

I would also like to name Rimma Karelskaya—a strong ballerina with an accomplished technique and a fine feeling of the classical line, and the young ballerina Lyudmila Bogomolova, who belongs to the type of *bravura* dancers. Bogomolova's excellent technique, her dynamic and expressive dancing and the elegance of her poses, have won her deserved recognition among the young ballerinas of the Bolshoi company. Among the first-class partners of almost all the ballerinas we should like to name Yuri Zhdanov, a *premier danseur* endowed with an excellent line and stage presence. *Romeo and Juliet, Swan Lake, Giselle, The Bronze Horseman* and many other ballets are in his repertoire.

No less interesting is the young growth of *danseurs nobles* at the Bolshoi. First and foremost there is Nikolai Fadeyechev. "Paris is captivated by Fadeyechev!" declared the French press at the time of the Bolshoi tour. He is to ballet what a tenor is to opera. But a dramatic tenor is even a greater rarity. Fadeyechev is just that. The noble nature of his movements is such, that no *bravura* or virtuosity dancing is called for, qualities which often win the sympathies of spectators for their own sake. The secret of Fadeyechev's success is much more subtle. He is a perfect lyrical hero. His every step gives authenticity to his portrayal: one cannot help loving and trusting him. As it befits a perfect lyrical hero, Fadeyechev is an excellent partner in supported adagio for his ballerina, a passionate lover in lyrical *pas de deux*. He has no equal at present in *Giselle* or *Swan Lake* at the Bolshoi.

Boris Khokhlov is different from Fadeyechev both in the style of execution and the style of his technique. Khokhlov is best in *tour de force* movements. Such is the nature of his talent. His jumps and tours are invariably applauded. Melancholic lyricism is not for him. In dancing he asserts the joy of living. His characters breathe warmth and animation, that is perhaps why he is so admirable in *Cinderella* and *Don Quixote*.

Gennady Ledyakh vies with Khokhlov (both are pupils of Asaf Messerer). Ledyakh is a strong dancer for whom no physical exertion is too much, it seems. His best roles are Basil in *Don Quixote*, Frondoso in *Laurencia*, the Prince in *Cinderella*. One sees him as a self-confident virile dancer inclined towards the loud and demonstrative *brio* style. Undoubtedly, Ledyakh may yet reveal great talent in character roles of a grotesque nature.

Gleb Yevdokimov has established himself as a very interesting classical and grotesque dancer. It is a pity that his stature does not allow him to take some leading roles, but in solos he invariably demonstrates clean-cut *batterie*, and lightness and virtuosity of classical technique which is a real pleasure to watch.

Two very young *danseuses* have caused quite a stir among the Bolshoi ballet lovers.

One is Yelena Ryabinkina, a pupil of Vera Vasilyeva, whose *début* was particularly in the news. A girl just out of ballet school, she made a tremendous success of the Odette-Odile part. Ryabinkina has eloquence in execution of the most complex steps from the arsenal of the *danse d'école*. But

67. Yaroslav Sekh (*Paganini*)

aside from that her precious gift is a clear and clever understanding of *what* she is performing. The youthful characters created by her are noble and pure. All this goes into the making of her character.

Yelena Ryabinkina has everything in store—the joy of "discovering" her own self and the world around her.

Katya Maximova is the other young *débutante*, quite justly considered to be the hope and pride of the Bolshoi. A pupil of Yelizaveta Gerdt, Maximova has fully grasped one of her teacher's main precepts: purity of dance form serves to create the image. Maximova's dancing is always so flawless that that in itself is a great gift. During the U.S.A. tour American audiences justly appraised Maximova's talent in *The Tale of the Stone Flower* in which she danced the role of her namesake Katerina. But she has one more quality that promises much: even the simplest and commonplace becomes poetic and inspired in her rendering. Everything acquires an inner charm. This became particularly evident in her Giselle prepared under the great Ulanova. Maximova's talent already manifests a quality so dear to Soviet art—an ability to assert the beauty of man, his emotions and aspirations, through the beauty of dance.

Vladimir Vasilyev (pupil of Mikhail Gabovich) is still very young, but already a fine artist. He started his career with the part of Danila in *The Tale of the Stone Flower*, appearing in that role on tours abroad. His style of dancing and his very looks are endearingly Russian, which can also be said of Katya Maximova. The warmth with which he performed the part, his engaging softness of motion and gesture, and the lyricism of his dancing promoted him to first ranks in the role of Danila. Vasilyev is endowed with a good elevation and, what is even more rare, considerable *ballon*. He soars in the air in broad extended leaps, his tours are excellent. Above all his style of dancing is strong and virile. He promises to become an excellent partner in supported adagio. A dancer of this type is a real acquisition for the company.

And finally in the 1961/62 season the Bolshoi Ballet company was joined by two graduates of the Moscow Ballet School—Natalya Bessmertnova and Mikhail Lavrovsky, a son of the ballet-master Leonid Lavrovsky. In her very first appearances in *Chopiniana* and *Pages from Life*, Natalya Bessmertnova displayed a nobility of manner and subtlety of execution. She has a long, soaring leap, and arms that seem "fluid". Mikhail Lavrovsky dances the important part of Philippe in *The Flames of Paris* with such youthful ingenuity and ardour and at the same time so lyrically that he immediately attracted notice.

As differing from most companies abroad, Soviet ballet increasingly cultivates what is customarily given the name of "character dance". This is an important sphere of stage dancing, closely related to and often merging with the sphere of classical academic dancing. Leading characters of new ballets are more often than not moulded with the help of steps borrowed not only and not so much from the classical dance as from character dances. Indeed, who would undertake to determine what predominates in the part of the Archer from Fokine's celebrated *Polovtsian Dances*? Only a great classical dancer can perform the part, though by far not all are suited for it.

Yaroslav Sekh is equally at home in both these elements. The story of his stage career is typical for our country. He attended a trade school in Lvov, and went in for dancing in his spare time appearing in amateur shows. He attracted notice and was sent first to a local ballet studio and then to the Moscow Bolshoi School. On graduation Sekh became solo dancer of the Bolshoi Theatre. His talent began to sparkle in character dances of old and contemporary ballets (his Young Gypsy in the tempestuous dance from act 2 of *The Tale of the Stone Flower* is unforgettable), and also in

68. Yelena Ryabinkina and Nikolai Fadeyechev *(Swan Lake)*

roles calling for a subtle psychological rendering. Such was Georgi, the friend and jealous lover without a rival from *Gayaneh*. The rendering of this role by Sekh proved how great are his creative resources. There was nothing fortuitous in Lavrovsky entrusting him with the deeply psychological role of Paganini in the Rachmaninov ballet of the same name, and Sekh created a strong character of great impact.

Yaroslav Sekh is representative of a whole group of character dancers. Mention must be made of Vladimir Levashov. He is known as one of the best interpreters of Mercutio, Shuraleh, and is particularly admired as Severyan in *The Tale of the Stone Flower*. His rendering of this character, ruthless and violent in the true spirit of Bazhov's fairy-tale, merits the highest possible praise. Levashov is a dancer-actor, one of the finest artists of the Bolshoi.

Happy is the theatre possessing "dancing actors" of this calibre. And there are so many of them in the company of the Bolshoi!

The Bolshoi Theatre is famed not only for its soloists, but for its brilliant *corps de ballet*, or, as it is customary to say, ensemble.

High standard of technique, perfect alignment and grouping, inspired and dramatic expressiveness in presentation of the most complicated situations in the action—such are the well recognised qualities of this ensemble. It is not accidental that during the Bolshoi tours abroad it was written of its *courps de ballet* that it "sparkled with stars".

69. Yekaterina Maximova *(The Tale of the Stone Flower)*

THE BALLET REPERTOIRE

In the last few years the Bolshoi Theatre has staged over twenty ballets, a good half of which were created by Soviet masters of the ballet.

To the Bolshoi—leading among the theatres in our capital—falls the honourable duty of demonstrating the best achievements of Soviet opera and ballet generally, and not just its own. That is why we see in the repertoire several Leningrad-produced ballets (*The Fountain of Bakhchisarai, Laurencia, Romeo and Juliet*, etc.) and some operas, which were first shown elsewhere (*Jalil, War and Peace*, and others).

The Bolshoi Theatre repertoire reflects the variety of creative searches of the entire Soviet ballet, with its abundance of themes, styles, choreographers' and composers' personalities, and performers' individual manner. Petipa may be found here alongside with Zakharov, Gorsky with Lavrovsky, Chabukiani with Vainonen, Fokine with Goleizovsky, Radunsky with Messerer, and Sergeyev with Grigorovich.

Soviet choreography endeavours to embrace a wider field of subject-matter, to find a greater diversity of expressive means and encourage individual seekings. What it needs most for further development is an unremitting competition of creative opinion, taste, style, genre preferences and so on and so forth. For however great the talent of any given choreographer or composer, his sole and exclusive rule over a ballet theatre is in the long run detrimental to art.

The oldest ballet in the Bolshoi repertoire is *Giselle*, first performed in 1844. Conceived by the genius of the French people it has that very rare and elusive quality—a remarkable unity of all components, that makes for a strong dramatic alloy. Tchaikovsky called *Giselle* a poetic, musical and dancing gem. In composing his own works he read and reread Adam's score. In *Giselle*, music, book and dances form a single whole. It is a specimen of perfect development of action towards its climax. The characters are simply yet subtly depicted. The somewhat naive melodies blend with the emotional reactions of *Giselle*'s heroes. The choreographic pattern is so conceived that it furthers and develops the dramatic plot. All the characters, all the important situations develop through dance. The second act with its romantic *ballet blanc* knows no equal. And all this serves one profound idea, never failing to move the spectator—that love is stronger than death.

In the sixties of the last century *Giselle* was on its way to disappearing from the stages of the world. To say that Russian ballet saved it from oblivion would be to belittle the importance of

70. Lyudmila Bogomolova in "Swan Princess" concert number (music by P. Tchaikovsky, choreography by V. Varkovitsky)
71. Boris Khokhlov (*Swan Lake*)
72. Shamil Yagudin in "Eroica" concert number to A. Skriabin's music (choreography by K. Goleizovsky)
73. Vladimir Levashov as Mercutio (*Romeo and Juliet*)

what it did. It raised the creation of Gautier, Saint-Georges, Perrot, Coralli and Adam to new heights and completely transformed it. Generation after generation of our choreographers and dancers enriched the dance treasury of *Giselle* and enhanced its content. Petipa, revering *Giselle* from his youth, considerably developed the action as expressed by choreography in the second act. Fokine and Gorsky introduced their own fine touches in the general scenic action. Asafiev made delicate changes in the instrumentation. Lavrovsky in his production of *Giselle* introduced excellent nuances of directing in the old version of the *corps de ballet* scenes of the first act.

In other words the present Russian *Giselle* is very much different from the French *Giselle* of the last century.

In the Russian version the emphasis gradually shifted from the first act to the second. The main theme is no longer the melodramatic story of a seduced maiden, as it was a hundred years ago. Glorification of love that conquers death has now become the *leitmotif* of *Giselle*. The Wilis are no longer depicted as avengers, but as judges of those who pushed Giselle to her grave. The heroes' love is tested at the fantastic nocturnal gathering of the Wilis. They pass the test and win the sympathy of the audiences of all times and nations.

Soviet ballerinas have endowed Giselle with such a yearning for happiness, that it runs through even the most tragic episodes of the ballet. Of particular depth and novelty is Ulanova's interpretation of the role.

The revised Petipa version of *Giselle* returned to the Paris Opéra and later was included in the repertoire of most of the ballet companies of the world.

A special place among the old ballets is occupied by *Don Quixote* (music by Ludwig Minkus). The ballet was first staged at the Bolshoi 92 years ago, in 1869. It is customary to speak of *Don Quixote* with a condescending smile. Indeed it has many imperfections. The story of the Knight of the Doleful Countenance served the composer and the author of the book merely as a pretext to show some unconnected scenes, describing the amusing love story of an innkeeper's daughter and a barber. And yet, despite all its shortcomings, the ballet continues to live and bring joy to spectators and performers, although both are perfectly aware of all its weak spots. A choreographer of great imagination, Gorsky endowed the dances with such passion, colour and rhythm that the audiences are captivated and forget their exasperation with the story.

There is probably no other ballet of the classic heritage that contains such a festive parade of classic and *demi-charactère* dancing as in the first act of *Don Quixote*. The clever interplay of alternating ensemble and solo dances, classic and character, lyrical and comical, grotesque and parody, makes this old ballet a classic, at least the best parts of it.

It is not surprising, therefore, that its influence has spread, as so many invisible threads, to new ballets. The first act as staged by Gorsky showed choreographers how to portray the people as the hero of a ballet, and thus assisted them in their searches.

French ballet music of the latter part of the nineteenth century is represented by two classical scores of Delibes.

Coppélia was first staged in Moscow in the 1880s. With it live—in some cases changed beyond recognition, in others, in much developed form—the creative methods of Saint-Léon, its choreographer. Delibes was held in high esteem by Tchaikovsky, while Glasunov counselled composers to study Delibes' scores as a model of co-ordination between music and the development of ballet action. Delibes' music is full of national humour and warmth. He shows profound sympathy for the folklore of Poland, Western Ukraine and Hungary, something rather rare for his day. In old ballets the artificial often obscured the natural and human. Delibes managed to avoid this even in a story about toys and dolls. He depicted his characters lovingly and humorously, making them both lyrical and comic. The comparatively few dramatic situations were expressively conveyed through music.

Many Russian choreographers invested something of their own fantasy into *Coppélia*. It is a pity, however, that the Bolshoi revivers of *Coppélia* have departed from its former story, and with it— from the literary source of the ballet. This has impaired the score. Their methods of production also do not always serve towards improvement of the classic composition.

An interesting bit of work has been done on another Delibes ballet, *Sylvia*. Because of its exceptionally trite story it failed to carve a lasting niche for itself on the stage. Attempts to overcome the existing discrepancies between music and action yielded no results, although the task was tackled by such choreographers as Lev Ivanov, Pavel Gerdt and partly by Fokine. It is true, though, that foreign masters of the ballet in the past century also failed in their endeavours to make *Sylvia* a deserving success.

Twenty-five years ago choreographer Leonid Lavrovsky together with the Leningrad theatre director and historian Vladimir Solovyov resorted to George Sand's *La Petite Fadette* in their search for a new subject to be used with the *Sylvia* music. The authors of the new ballet were forgiven the liberties they took with the score (part of it remained altogether unused) because they succeeded in creating a bold and moving production.

The story of *Fadetta* is laid in a French village in mid-19th century. The villagers are hounding the family of the old beggar Ursula, who lives in the woods. Fadetta, Ursula's sixteen-year-old granddaughter, is a wilful, wild and mischievous girl who hates her tormentors. She changes her mind about people when she meets André, a farmer's son. He is the first person to treat her as a human being. The climax is extremely dramatic. André invites Fadetta to a village *fête*. The old farmer raises his hand against his son and his sweetheart. The whole village turns against André. He disowns his father and leaves with Fadetta to look for happiness elsewhere.

The ballet theatre had never known such a democratic and rebellious theme yet. The development of the characters was carried out in a new way that brought out the underlying idea of the whole work. Lavrovsky proved himself here a past master of dance characterisation. The dance monologues and dialogues created by him were profoundly psychological, unprecedentedly so.

The authenticity of feelings thus expressed enriched the traditional ballet forms and made them as convincing as a play on the legitimate stage. It was this that imbued *Fadetta* with new significance and merited its revival on the stage of the Bolshoi Filial.

Lavrovsky gained wide recognition by developing in *Romeo and Juliet* the new ideas he had outlined in *Fadetta*.

Tchaikovsky's great trio of ballets has had the run of the Bolshoi stage for many years now in different choreographic versions. Tchaikovsky's ballets do not require our recommendation. Their universal significance is well known. Music from them is heard over the radio almost daily, and fragments from them are often shown on television. Thirty-three Soviet ballet theatres, 19 ballet schools and thousands of amateur dance groups regularly stage these ballets or fragments from them. Composers turn to Tchaikovsky when creating new themes and images, for they regard his works as a reliable textbook, capable of answering many theoretical and practical questions. To the masters of our ballet Tchaikovsky's works are just as much a school of psychological realism as Chekhov's are for our writers and Stanislavsky's for our actors.

Alongside Tchaikovsky's ballets proudly stands Glasunov's *Raymonda* (1896-97). Countess Raymonda lives in a Provence castle. Her fiancée Jean de Brienne is away on a crusade. Abderrahman, a Saracen chieftain, arrives in his absence. Raymonda's beauty fills him with a desire to carry her away. He almost succeeds, but Jean de Brienne returns unexpectedly and defeats him in violent combat. The last act shows the wedding festivities.

The musical dramaturgy of the ballet is built on the principle of contrasting dance suites, different in genre. Petipa and Glasunov contrasted a suite of classical dances to that of *danse de charactère*. The serenity of Raymonda's lyrical world clashes with the untrammeled vehemence of the Saracen's passion. The struggle between the motifs of the classical and the Spanish and Moorish dances is cleverly brought out in the music, as it was conceived by the choreographer. These two worlds meet in the first act and clash again in the second. Hungarian dances enter the choreographic pattern with Raymonda's lover who saves her from the Saracen. The third act is an original interweaving of rhythms and imagery of classical dancing with Hungarian folk ones. Thus was born the famous *grand pas classique hongroise*—an undying example of how folk dances can be adapted in classical ballet, a touchstone for *premiers danseurs* and *danseuses*.

Together with *The Sleeping Beauty*, Petipa's *Raymonda* is part of the treasury of classical dance, its voluminous encyclopaedia. In the Oriental dancing *fête* of the second act of *Raymonda* the composer developed what was achieved by Borodin's *Polovtsian Dances* and Glinka's Oriental dances from the fourth act of *Ruslan and Lyudmila*. *Raymonda* has an especial appeal to the numerous performers of character dances.

Lavrovsky, who is the current producer of *Raymonda* at the Bolshoi, has retained whole fragments of the Petipa and Gorsky choreography.

Fokine's *Les Sylphides (Chopiniana)*, known all over the world, has a place of its own at the Bolshoi alongside with these classics.

We see that the classical heritage occupies a place of honour in the repertoire of the Bolshoi, but Soviet ballets are more numerous.

The earliest of Soviet ballets, *Red Poppy*, is now over thirty years old. In 1949 Lavrovsky created a new version, which received a new title—*Red Flower*.

In the revised story and production many archaic scenes of the 1927 version were weeded out, and the ballet acquired an excellent new character in the person of Ma Li-chen, hero-leader of the coolies. The character of the heroine Tao Hoa was considerably enriched. She now became partisan of the struggle for freedom and happiness of her country. Mass scenes—always Lavrovsky's strong point—acquired three-dimensional expressiveness which was lacking before. The changes made in the *Red Poppy* by the Bolshoi made possible a revival of this ballet on many other stages of the Soviet Union.

Next after the *Red Flower* came *The Flames of Paris* produced at the Bolshoi in 1933 by choreographer Vasily Vainonen. The best in this ballet is its third act. Here Asafiev brought to life a world of images new to the ballet—the dance and song of the *sans-culottes* of the French revolutionary era. Their intonations called for the creation of a new and original dance idiom, one imbued with national humour, excitement, wrath and thirst for struggle. The third act shows Parisians, soldiers of the Marseilles battalion, people from the provinces. The spectators see dances from Auvergne and Marseilles, so well done and with such understanding of the very substance of French folk dancing that Vainonen's choreography seems to have been copied from nature. But the main thing is still ahead—the Basque dance. It is more than just a folk dance, it is a march, a hymn filled with intonations calling people to battle. The choreographer created new plastic accents, sharp springing movements, abrupt gestures of muscular arms. The dance grows into a powerful symbol. It is the spark that sets Paris aflame. The call "Ça ira" is heard, giving birth to a magnificent image of people in revolt, people still oppressed but already invincible.

There are choreographic gems in other acts as well. Such is the *pas de quatre* by the three Marseillais and Jeanne in the first act. Characteristic poses and movements, transforming the classical *pas* and lending them new colour, create expressive portraits of the four dancing the quartet. Then there is Cupid in the court theatre presentation—a deliberate parody on the Rococo style. The grand *pas de deux* of the Marseillais and Jeanne is an excellent composition, often performed at recitals.

The best dances of this ballet show that the seemingly unmalleable academic *pas* are quite capable of taking on new elements and that a bold, imaginative choreographer can endow them with new content. They also show that there is no controversy between classical and character dancing, if both serve the main purpose—the creation of an image.

It is exactly twenty-five years ago that *The Fountain of Bakhchisarai* was first produced. The subject-matter of Pushkin's poem is told in ballet form in an interesting way. As differing from the poem, the ballet starts with the scene of a *fête* at the castle of Maria's father, a Polish magnate. Ensemble dances are interspersed with Maria's eloquent duets with Waclaw, full of lyricism and youthful emotion. At the very height of festivities the castle is attacked by Tatars. Maria's father and friends are killed. Waclaw dies defending her against Khan Girei. The scene shifts to Girei's harem. His return is eagerly awaited by his favourite wife Zarema. But Girei is a changed man. All his thoughts are of Maria whom he brought to Bakhchisarai after the raid on Poland. From a fierce khan he has become a slave of love and this love has elevated him to a higher moral plane.

The ballet reflects the poet's thought that love and violence are incompatible, that true love is all-conquering. The romantic form of expression, which distinguishes Pushkin's earlier works, accords full well with the poetical nature of the art of dancing.

The joint creative labour of composer Boris Asafiev, choreographer Rostislav Zakharov, designer of the settings and costumes Valentina Khodasevich, and others made this production, if not quite flawless, then at least novel and exemplary in many respects. Its secret lies in the unity and harmony of the choreographic drama, which is not found in all the works from the classical heritage by far. Once this unity has been attained, a ballet is ensured a long and lasting scenic life, despite weaknesses of some of its separate parts.

Boris Asafiev's perfect understanding of ballet dramaturgy, his skilful use of "speaking pauses" inherited from the ballet music of the past, his clear-cut ideological and artistic conception of the production, and his awareness of what is good theatre—all this makes the music of *The Fountain of Bakhchisarai* what it is. We are grateful to Asafiev for linking Soviet ballet with classical literature—with Pushkin, Gogol and Balzac. He taught musicians how to interpret original literary works. And at the same time, through his scores, he gave composers and choreographers a series of lessons on correlation between the component parts of a ballet. His collaboration with Nikolai Volkov, author of many ballet books from *The Flames of Paris* to *Spartacus*, was most fruitful. Volkov's detailed book for *The Fountain of Bakhchisarai* is an excellent example of drama conceived with a view to its choreographic rendering.

The Fountain of Bakhchisarai was Rostislav Zakharov's début as choreographer. His mises-en-scène are austere and new. The intensely psychological dancing conveys a content that heretofore seemed out of the ballet's reach. His third act is still an unmatched example of the art of ballet directing. Zakharov clearly saw the logic of dramatic development and succeeded in building up a convincing climax through mises-en-scène penetrating into the "core" of the image and the action. The Fountain of Bakhchisarai captivates the audiences by the psychological realism of its characters. They change, they grow—in other words, they portray the flow of passions and emotions.

The Fountain of Bakhchisarai has become a Soviet classic. It marked the beginning of Ulanova's brilliant career. It also brought fame to many dancers in Moscow: to Gusev and Smoltsov (as Girei), Gabovich (as Waclaw), Asaf Messerer (as Nurali), Sulamith Messerer and Natalya Konius (as Zarema).

Work on roles in The Fountain of Bakhchisarai is an excellent school of acting. It makes one ponder on the psychological content of a ballet role. The Fountain of Bakhchisarai wrote a new page into the history of Soviet ballet. Like Fadetta, it concentrated the attention of choreographers and performers on man's inner world, on his noble feelings and thoughts. There is no theatre in the Soviet Union that does not stage this popular ballet.

Quite different from The Fountain of Bakhchisarai is the ballet Laurencia (music by Alexander Krein, choreographer Vakhtang Chabukiani) so called after the heroine of Lope de Vega's famous tragedy Fuenteovejuna. These two ballets, forming part of the same repertoire, speak not only of variety of genres, but also of Soviet ballet's wide search for solutions of major themes.

Chabukiani peopled this production with characters who all have their own convincing dance imagery. The heroes—Laurencia and Frondoso—are the most true-to-life, expressive and attractive of these. Chabukiani always endeavours to show his heroes in motion and in action. He likes to develop his characters in the course of the ballet. Gestures and mimed mises-en-scène are usually avoided by him. Dance is the choreographer's primary element of expression.

The entire story is told in the language of the dance—lively, animated, stirring and passionate. And although there are considerable shortcomings (the book is too primitive and the direction at times inadequate), the audiences nevertheless enter the world of the clear and eloquent classical dance. Krein's music fits the dramatic tension of the ballet well. As composer Dmitry Kabalevsky said, "at times it is truly symphonic and at the same time extremely theatrical".

Critics are unanimous in classing Laurencia a festival of the dance. Such are the strong points of this ballet which has been a sort of touchstone for several generations of dancers. Plisetskaya, Struchkova, Kondratov, Ledyakh and many other experienced dancers and beginners revealed their talents in this ballet and discovered for themselves new angles of their own gifts.

The Bronze Horseman belongs to the category of monumental ballets in the repertoire of the Bolshoi. It was first produced in 1949, on the 150th anniversary of Pushkin's birth.

The ballet makes no claim to any comparison with the poem. Pushkin's philosophical idea is there, but it is not made the main theme. It is a sort of scenic illustration to the poem, glorifying the beauty of St. Petersburg, of its white nights extolled by Pushkin and Dostoyevsky, of the Bronze Horseman monument and the beauty of Pushkin's verse. It would have been more correct to call the ballet Yevgeny and Parasha, inasmuch as it deals chiefly with the personal drama of these two young lovers.

Masters of Soviet ballet portrayed their hero Yevgeny with much love. Some of them depicted him as a romantic lover who has suffered misfortune, others as a downtrodden and humiliated man who sees in his love for Parasha the only justification of a hard life, yet others presented him as a naive young man losing his reason in a moment of trial, but in his madness cursing all human misery on earth.

Glière's music constitutes an important part of the ballet. The composer skilfully blends symphonic music and traditional ballet forms. Those parts of the score which speak of the greatest hero—Petersburg, Peter the Great, the Bronze Horseman, are well known aside from the stage: they are often rendered at symphony concerts, over the radio and television. The symphonic elaboration of the main theme of the Bronze Horseman adds dramatic impact to the ballet, assisting us in the understanding of its underlying idea.

The ballet (produced by Zakharov with settings by Professor Bobyshov), is very spectacular. It captures one's imagination from the very start—from the first scenes showing the building of the town on the Neva, the arrival of Peter the Great, the landscape of the Summer Garden, the Neva embankments, the Petrovsky Palace. The best scene of the ballet is in the courtyard of Parasha's home. Here there is much that is new and appealing. Pretty Russian girls dance in a ring and play games and the innocence and light-heartedness of these games contrast well with the impending tragedy.

Not since the days of *Le Corsaire* has the Bolshoi stage seen such stirring scenes as the flood in *The Bronze Horseman*. The crowd rushes frantically about the Neva embankment as the waters overflow the river banks, inundate the square, foaming and raging around the buildings and the monument to Peter the Great. People perish in the waters; wreckages and boats float across the stage—the picture of a terrible flood is complete.

Quite different in character and genre is the ballet *Mirandolina* (music by Sergei Vasilenko, choreography by Vasily Vainonen), first staged at the Bolshoi Filial in 1949. This excellently presented ballet version of Goldoni's *La Locandiera* is charming in its humour and variety of scenes.

Another ballet that has proved highly successful with Muscovites is *Shuraleh*, choreographed by Leonid Yacobson to music of the talented young Tatar composer Yarullin, who was killed in the Great Patriotic War. *Shuraleh* has been running at the Bolshoi since 1955 and is vastly popular. The secret of its success lies in the interesting story adapted from a classic fairy-tale by the Tatar writer Tukai, in its use of Tatar folklore, in the colourful music and original methods of production. The choreography of the second act is particularly admirable. While some of our choreographers are inclined to overuse mime, Yacobson's field of action has always been the dance. He builds up his characters through dance idiom. The wedding feast is used as a chance to present a great many dances inspired by Tatar folklore. It is full of humorous or lyrical scenes, at times a little sad, but mostly uproariously merry. Together they form a colourful motley picture. Matchmakers, bridesmaids, best men and the parents of the hero—all are just like people anywhere else, yet with their own inimitable national colour.

In *Shuraleh* the audiences were introduced to the young ballerina Marina Kondratyeva. Yuri Gofman, an experienced actor and dancer, gave a very fresh performance as Batyr, sharing the success with Yuri Kondratov, the other dancer in the same role.

74. *Giselle*, scene from act 1
75. Galina Ulanova and Vladimir Preobrazhensky (act 2)
76-81. Galina Ulanova and Nikolai Fadeyechev (act 1)
82. Maya Samokhvalova as Myrtha *(Giselle)*

DON QUIXOTE
83. Variations (Vera Mitrayeva)
84. Matador (Sergei Koren)

83

84

SWAN LAKE
85. Scene from act 1
86. Scene from act 2
87. Hungarian Dance (Yadviga Sangovich and Sergei Koren)
88. Scene from act 4
89. Maya Plisetskaya as Odette

90

91

92

93

RAYMONDA
90. Raymonda and Jean de Brienne (Yelena Ryabinkina and Nikolai Fadeyechev)
91. Yelena Ryabinkina as Raymonda
92. Mazurka performed by Yadviga Sangovich and Vladimir Kudryashov
93. Maya Plisetskaya as Raymonda
94. Yelena Ryabinkina and Alexander Begak as Raymonda and Abdrakhman
95-96. Spanish Dance (Yelena Kholina and Yaroslav Sekh)
97. Saracen Dance (Elmira Kosterina and Georgi Farmanyants)

CHOPINIANA
98. Galina Ulanova, Nikolai Fadeyechev, Rimma Karelskaya
99-102. Galina Ulanova and Nikolai Fadeyechev

THE FOUNTAIN OF BAKH-
CHISARAI

103. Maya Plisetskaya as Zarema
104. Marianna Bogolyubskaya and Pyotr Gusev as Maria and Girei
105. Dance of the Harem
106. Alexander Lapauri as Girei
107. Marina Kolpakchi as Zarema

THE FLAMES OF PARIS
108-109. Nina Timofeyeva performing *adagio*, act 4
110. Georgi Farmanyants as Filippe

We now come to Prokofiev's three ballets: *Cinderella*, first staged at the Bolshoi in 1945, *Romeo and Juliet*, produced here in 1946, and *The Tale of the Stone Flower*, produced in the present version in 1959.

Prokofiev dedicated *Cinderella* to Tchaikovsky, often saying that it was inspired by *The Sleeping Beauty*. Whether intentionally or not, there is something of Tchaikovsky in the music, which in no way lessens that which is Prokofiev's inimitably own. His individual qualities are reflected in the philosophical development of his musical thought, in the expansion and enhancement of the lyrical and melodious aspects of the music. In the score the leading role is played by strings, and that is something unusual for Prokofiev. Inspired by Tchaikovsky, Prokofiev has composed some splendid waltzes, beautiful in their tuneful melody. And that was something new too for there are very few waltzes in Prokofiev's earlier compositions for ballet.

Prokofiev, whose music was always forceful and at times sharply rhythmical, composed some soft, lyrical melodies for *Cinderella*. His gift for depicting sharp and bitingly grotesque characteristics enabled him to draw a vivid picture of the Court, of the evil stepmother and of the stupid and selfish Ugly Sisters.

The composer painted with great sympathy and love the image of Cinderella herself, a girl with a noble heart. Both *Romeo and Juliet* and *Cinderella* show how fruitful was Prokofiev's assimilation of classical traditions.

There are ballets which bring success to all their creators—author of the book, composer, choreographer and artist. Others owe their success to some one factor—either music, or dance. The brilliant music in *Cinderella* overshadows both the talented and inventive directing of Zakharov and the settings by the remarkable Soviet artist Pyotr Williams. For all that, Zakharov's and Williams' work is undoubtedly spectacular and striking. It is enough to recall the scene at the ball when Cinderella hurries home as the clock strikes twelve. The moving panorama settings create the illusion that the scene is changing. The Prince's journey round the world in search of the owner of the glass slipper shows the artist's rare inventiveness. The transformation scene of act one, in which the walls of Cinderella's home melt to reveal the changing seasons of the year, also leaves an indelible impression.

We shall not try to compare *Cinderella* with *Romeo and Juliet*. There is too big a gap between Perrault's fairy-tale and Shakespeare's tragedy, between the theme of virtue rewarded and the theme of mortal feud of two ages.

Romeo and Juliet has already gained world popularity. It has been popularised by symphony orchestras, radio broadcasts, long-playing records, and the ballet-film which, incidentally, is inferior to the original stage production.

Romeo and Juliet is an epoch-making phenomenon. It shows that ballet has acquired new qualities without which it would have been impossible to present Shakespeare on the choreographic stage.

For two whole centuries choreographers and dancers the world over dreamed of staging Shakespeare. Legends have reached us of the "passionate pantomime" *Romeo og Giulietta* of the Danish choreographer Galeotti, of the Petersburg ballet *Romeo i Yulia* choreographed by Ivan Valberg to music by Steibelt. In those same years Vigano, much lauded by Stendhal, was creating his Shakespeare ballets.

This task proved too difficult. The war waged by England's genius against medieval bondage and cruelty, his hymn to the freedom of spirit and humanism, were alien to aristocratic ballet *habitués*. The fact that the rehearsals of *Macbeth* as a ballet, started in Russia by Didelot, were interrupted in 1825, was rather a significant one. At the same time picturesque and opulent *féeries* wherein stories, borrowed from Shakespeare, served as a purely external pretext, flourished everywhere. There were a great many extravaganzas "adapted" from Shakespeare's plays, staged in Paris, Berlin, Vienna and Milan.

Tchaikovsky, a great lover of ballet and a brilliant interpreter of Shakespeare in music, flatly refused to compose ballet music for *The Tempest*. "The story of *The Tempest* is too big and too deep for a ballet," he wrote to the man who was engaged on the book. "I simply cannot imagine Miranda or Ferdinand doing *battements, entrechats,* etc." Sad as it may sound, Tchaikovsky was right: the ballet of those days could not have coped with Shakespeare's themes, for it did not possess the means of bringing out his thoughts.

Let there be no mistake. The task is not at all to translate Shakespeare into the language of the dance. Such vulgar understanding of the problem can only lead to ludicrous results. The task is neither to relate Shakespeare's stories, nor to render his plots in dance terms. The first is impossible in ballet, the second is insufficient both for Shakespeare and for the art of dancing.

Faithfulness to Shakespeare is above all faithfulness to his ideas and images and not to the sequence of stage situations. This called for a totally new approach, and it was the Soviet ballet that found and developed this new approach in the process of staging Pushkin.

Working on Pushkin our ballet learned to build up the leading characters and develop them throughout the entire action. In *Romeo and Juliet* the development of images acquired a new quality. Juliet's mood in the ball scene changes three times—the listlessness she displays dancing with Paris is followed by trepidation that gives way to joy when she meets the stranger, and then to heart-rending alarm as she learns that he is the son of a mortal enemy.

Armed with Shakespeare's realistic method, the authors of *Romeo and Juliet* (Prokofiev, Lavrovsky, Radlov, Williams), succeeded in re-creating the entire gamut of dramatic action of the play: we are shown much more than a development of the heroes' love story, we see the morals and passions of a whole epoch. Such reading of the tragedy (even opera composers of the 19th century did not dare interpret it in this manner) made it possible to bring out the main theme—the unequal struggle waged by the children of tomorrow against the injusticies of yesterday.

The clash between Tybalt and Mercutio, as depicted by Shakespeare, is much more than a duel of swords. The music in this scene reveals in the true Shakespearean way the struggle between the different outlooks of the opponents. It sounds melancholy and moving as Mercutio dies, as if saying farewell to him. The death of Tybalt is accompanied by pounding chords with menacing pauses. Just as Shakespeare himself wrote:

> The man that hath no music in himself
> Nor is not moved with concord of sweet sounds
> Is fit for treasons, stratagems and spoils;
> The motions of his spirit are dull as night . . . .

Praise is due to Lavrovsky not simply for creating such overwhelmingly powerful and impressive scenes as the duel between Mercutio and Tybalt (their roles were excellently performed by Koren and Yermolayev) but also for finding means whereby to interpret Shakespeare's grandiose ideas in terms of ballet.

The realism of Soviet ballet has helped to create yet another image, an image that is not among the list of characters, but one that Shakespeare obviously had in mind—the image of the people. Participation of the masses in the ballet elevated Romeo and Juliet's love to the heights of great symbolism—their love is like a banner in the struggle for the happiness of all who hate the sinister and departing world of blood-thirsty enmity.

Prokofiev's last ballet is *The Tale of the Stone Flower*. It might appear to some narrow-minded student of Prokofiev's works that here the composer departed from the principles on which he based his *Romeo and Juliet*. However, any attempt to draw a comparison between *Romeo and Juliet* and his preceding ballets is liable to arouse similar suspicions. The truth is that if *The Tale of the Stone Flower* has indeed been composed in a manner quite different to that of *Romeo and Juliet*, it was done so because of the author's extraordinary feeling for the new in art.

There are certain common traits in *Swan Lake* and *The Tale of the Stone Flower*. Both belong to the genre of lyrical song without words. Both are choreographic poems (and not dramas) singing love and nature. In both the classic dance is made to extoll the high moral qualities of human soul. However great are the common features—both in genre and content—they in no way belittle the incomparable individual beauty of Prokofiev's music. Perhaps more in *The Tale of the Stone Flower* than in his preceding ballets, his music acquires a classical purity, a simplicity and a depth of thought which make it akin to his Seventh Symphony.

The story of the ballet is very simple. Danila, a Urals stonecutter, is overwhelmed by a burning desire to make a perfect flower of stone. This passion brings him into the very bowels of the Copper Mountain, the domain of its Mistress—owner of fabulous subterrenean riches. She shows Danila the fantastic play of semiprecious stones. The stonecutter now dreams of nothing but these wonderful images, he forgets all and everything in his desire to re-create them in stone. Danila's sweetheart Katerina pines for her lost love. Severyan, the wicked overseer, tries to seduce Katerina. The Mistress of the Copper Mountain severely punishes Severyan for his cruelty to poor working people. Katerina meanwhile goes in search of Danila. She frees him from the bondage of the Mistress of the Copper Mountain and returns him to real life.

Yuri Grigorovich, the young choreographer, and Soliko Virsaladze, the artist, created a ballet of great originality in which everything, beginning with the *décor*, is full of poetry.

The entire stage is swathed in black velvet. In the background a dark green drop traced with light green veins imitates the lid of a malachite box. From time to time this lid is lifted, and we see behind it the setting for the scene. Sometimes it is a Urals landscape, then Danila's cottage, then again—the heart of the Copper Mountain, or the grounds of a fair. . . . The dancers seem to be coming out of the malachite box to the wide spaces of the stage where they are free to dance and act.

Thus in the scene of the Fair a motley festive crowd seems to tumble out of the box, possessed by the impetuous fervour of the Russian dance. A group of revellers headed by the lusty Severyan is particularly prominent. A gypsy dance follows. It breaks off at the sudden appearance of the Mistress of the Copper Mountain disguised as a simple peasant girl. Severyan goes in pursuit of her, but his feet stick to the ground. The girl takes the form of the formidable Mistress while Severyan gradually sinks into the earth.

The costumes, too, are eloquent. The friends of Katerina and Danila are dressed in soft pastel shades, and when Severyan, the villain, breaks into this world of simple love and friendship, the image of the evil destroyer of happiness is emphasised by the violent mauve of his shirt and deep black of his *poddyovka*.

Our critics highly praised the work of Grigorovich and Virsaladze and at the same time found quite a few faults. One must say in full justice that in any work of art the demerits leap to the eye at once, while the merits are fully appreciated only with time. *The Tale of the Stone Flower* should be seen and heard again and again, and every time will bring its beautiful discoveries in content and execution.

One can but rejoice that the ballet repertoire is now replenished with new ballets notable for their high musical merits.

Ballets by Aram Khachaturyan share a place of honour at the Bolshoi with the Prokofiev creations. Khachaturyan's scores bear the mark of his magnificent and passionate talent.

The story of how Spartacus, a Thracian, becoming a gladiator in slavery, rallied his friends for unequal struggle with the legions of all-powerful Rome, is well known. In antiquity, Khachaturyan found heroic imagery akin to contemporaneity in theme and spirit. The romantic exaltation and fervour of the music are overpowering. Khachaturyan mixed in his palette the colours of primitive pastorale, of pathetic sorrow, of militant heroism, of languid sensuality. The music of his *Spartacus* is spectacular and decorative. Its texture is intricately symphonic. The task of finding its choreographic counterpart is difficult, if not impossible.

The ballet is a grandiose pantomime with dances. It contains many excellent *mises-en-scène* by Moiseyev, scattered about the entire ballet. Such scenes as the triumphant march, as the gladiators' fights in the Coliseum, are first-class. In Leningrad this ballet has been staged by Leonid Yakobson. Muscovites first saw his version of *Spartacus* in the 1961-62 Bolshoi Theatre season.

Gayaneh, another ballet by Khachaturyan, has a long history. The Bolshoi gave it a new book and new choreography. Because of this the composer had to rewrite the score, half of which is new.

The action takes place in Armenia. Two hunter friends Armen and Georgi rescue Ayesha, a girl from a mountain village who got lost in a storm. We are then introduced to Gayaneh, who has been in love with Armen for a long time. The friends carry Ayesha into the village. Gayaneh nurses Ayesha, with whom Georgi falls in love. He is jealous of Armen, quite groundlessly, and quarrels with him. Later, when Armen is in trouble (he falls down a precipice) Georgi does not come to his help at once, and only the hunters, appearing by chance on the scene, save Armen from impending death.

Armen lost his sight. Georgi is tormented by conscience.

However, Armen regains his sight. Georgi admits that he has infringed on the sacred law of friendship. Armen forgives him, but the people (these dramatic events take place at the time of harvest festivities) are silent. Georgi brings out his own verdict: he leaves the village. Ayesha, who loves him, goes with him.

This plot, rather involved for a ballet, is far from flawless. The sudden recovery of Armen's sight is rather naive. Georgi appears too gullible at the beginning. Khachaturyan's outstanding music alone justifies the story, elevating it to the level of big and moving ideas.

Soviet ballet is concerned with the moral and aesthetic education of its spectators. It considers it a great honour and privilege to speak about the stirring problems of life. Such survivals of the dog-eat-dog psychology of the past in human conscience as egotism, jealousy, and disregard of duty invariably arouse the indignation of Soviet people. *Gayaneh* poses these problems of morals and ethics, and that is what makes this production really moving. Vasily Vainonen's choreography is far from even. However, he succeeded in tackling perhaps the most difficult task: that of creating psychological monologues and dialogues for Georgi, whose role is brilliantly rendered by Yaroslav Sekh. Vainonen's approach to the problem of revealing his heroes' inner world is invariably a choreographic one. They eloquently speak in the idiom of the dance. The dances depicting life at an Armenian collective farm are particularly colourful. The girls' parts are less interesting, though they do contain at times some dance features quite worthy of attention.

The Path of Thunder—ballet after the novel of the same title by the South-African author Peter Abrahams—had its *première* at the Bolshoi in June 1959. Abrahams' novel has stood several editions in the U.S.S.R., it has also been adapted for the drama, the opera and the cinema. The fate of Lanny, a coloured teacher, and Sarie, a white girl, who loved each other truly and were murdered by South-African racists made a moving impression on our audiences.

Kara Karayev's music makes a tremendous impact. A pupil of Dmitry Shostakovich, this Azerbaijanian composer dedicated his score to the memory of Sergei Prokofiev. Being a master of completely modern symphonic musical idiom, Karayev tells the tragic story of his heroes with tremendous temperament. His music passionately speaks of love—love for the heroes, love for mankind, love for the peoples of Africa, wakening up to struggle for freedom.

The theme of the fate of black peoples of Africa has been undertaken for the first time in Russian ballet. Every step means a new problem to the choreographer. Konstantin Sergeyev did not always succeed in finding an original rendering of dramatic situations, and his dances sometimes fall short of the desired passionate intensity. The important thing, however, is that he is invariably true to the novel and the music, asserting that love is the greatest gift of life, and extolling human dignity and honour, that are worthy of defending to the last breath. The scenes where the coloured hero and the white heroine meet are noted for their fresh choreographic approaches and intricate psychological undercurrent. The finale of the second act has been excellently conceived in the music and brilliantly rendered in dance form: genuine feeling destroys all barriers in its way, and breaks through racial prejudices, through the fear of loving and being loved. The choreography of the coloured maids' scene is very well done, and many of the ensemble dances are quite interesting.

Quite recently the Bolshoi produced two *premières*. One is the new three-act production of *The Little Humpbacked Horse*, and the other—one-act *Paganini*.

The Little Humpbacked Horse by Yershov is of the most popular Russian fairy-tales. The ballet *The Little Humpbacked Horse* created by Saint-Léon and later revised first by Petipa and then by Gorsky, has been running on the Russian stage for a little under a century. This old ballet, though abounding in choreographic merits, had some very serious defects.

The distortion of Yershov's fairy-tale was the major one. Suffice it to say that the Russian tsar of Yershov's tale was replaced in the ballet by some Oriental khan. The search for the Fire-bird was left out altogether, while Ivanushka—the symbol of folk wisdom—became almost a fool.

Pugni's music with various dances by other composers interposed, added nothing to the artistic merits of the production.

The authors of the new ballet brought it considerably closer to Yershov's original. The most successful component of this ballet is the music, written by the twenty-seven-year-old composer Rodion Shchedrin. It has been already recorded on LP records and is broadcast regularly. The composer possesses that rare gift of musical wittiness. Shchedrin is almost equally at home with humour and satire, genre and fantastic scenes. His musical idiom rings a modern and colourful note. Shchedrin laughs heartily at all that is worth a laugh and at the same time arouses the audience's sympathies for his heroes. His musical sense of character is highly commendable.

Alexander Radunsky, choreographer and wonderful performer of the tsar's role, has dispayed much imagination in this ballet. The comic and burlesque scenes are his best and fetch a big laugh. The clever and quick Ivanushka though seemingly obeying all the tsar's whims and orders gets the better of him all the time. And when it comes to the Tsar-Maid, Ivanushka, told to steal her for the tsar, makes her his own bride instead.

It is quite natural that children adore this fairy-tale ballet.

First shown in the past season was Lavrovsky's one-act ballet *Paganini*. He radically changed the original version of this ballet, created by Fokine to Rachmaninov's music.

Lavrovsky built his ballet around the conflict between the inspired personality of Paganini and the world of reactionary clerics and jealous rivals. Paganini could have died only physically. Spiritually, he will live for ever in his immortal creations . . . . This idea has been carried out emphatically in the new production.

Yaroslav Sekh's excellent rendering of the title role, and Vadim Ryndin's settings are particularly noteworthy.

During the 1960-61 season the Bolshoi presented *Forest Song* with music by Hermann Zhukovsky and book by Mikhail Gabovich, staged by Alexander Lapauri and Olga Tarasova, and *City at Night*, music by Béla Bartók, book and production by Leonid Lavrovsky.

Of considerable interest was the *début* of Vladimir Vasilyev and Natalya Kasatkina as ballet-masters who produced the one-act ballet *Vanina Vanini* (libretto by the producers after Stendhal's story, music by N. Karetnikov).

The first ballet production of the 1961-62 season was *Pages from Life*, music by Andrei Balanchivadze, book and production by Leonid Lavrovsky.

Years of travel have brought universal recognition to the Bolshoi Theatre. Today it continues its search for new ballets and new authors, as well as new media of expression. The company has all the talent it needs for accomplishing this task.

OUR POINT OF VIEW

Quite often in the foreign press we find something like the following reasoning: the Soviet ballet is a replica of the ballet of the Imperial theatres; its devotion to the "Petipa tradition" (the entire picture of Russian ballet in the past century is obscured without any justification by this name alone) smacks of conservatism; the Soviet Union—the country of great revolutionary reforms—for some reason avoids them in ballet. The reader is offered the following *cliché*: West-European and American ballet evolved from the "revolutionary reforms" of Fokine and his successors, reforms, effected in Diaghilev's "Saisons Russes" in Paris and London and *not* in Russia. Soviet ballet, on the contrary, he is told, evolved from the Petipa "Imperial traditions" ignoring the modern innovations of Fokine and other "revolutionaries" of the dance.

What are the aims of ballet? What are its vital interests? What do we mean by tradition and innovation in this branch of art? A correct answer to these questions will enable one to properly evaluate the progress of ballet—both in the Soviet Union and abroad.

* * *

In the second half of the last century ballet in Western Europe was considered to be entertainment *par excellence*. It was there for amusement, to give one's brains a rest. Ballet had to present beautiful lines of the female body, graceful poses and groups, feats of dance virtuosity and bodily training. Some genre scenes were allowed—they had to be exotic or burlesque, and could be done in the idiom of character or grotesque dance.

Any connection with real life, any subject speaking of man and his destiny, in other words, anything that comprises the very essence of drama, all this was ruled out for ballet and considered completely out of place.

One was told that ballet in its highest manifestations required no story. It was not meant to "depict" or "contain" anything. The most that was required of it was to give the "stars" a chance to appear. Diversity of impressions—that was what really mattered in ballet. Diversity of impressions should be strived for in everything—from the settings and costumes to the very dance patterns. The choreographer had to keep inventing something new to thrill the sophisticated audience.

91

As a result of this, ballet became something of a recital in costume. The difference between ballet, variety programmes and the circus became practically nonexistent. All these served one and the same purpose: to help people kill time with a minimum of spiritual effort.

Spectacles of this kind certainly please the eye. But they fail to stir the heart and mind.

And so it happened that willingly or not ballet severed its union with other arts. In the best of cases literature and music were made into mere servants of the dance. The educational value of such art is almost nil, nor has it anything to narrate. Mime and pantomime, redundant unless there is a motivated story, disappeared altogether. Ballet of this kind could not, with all justice, bear the name of Art. It inevitably degenerated into a craft.

Similar phenomena were taking place in Russia's Imperial theatres, with the only difference that full-length monumental ballets were maintained for the sake of tradition. Western Europe preferred brief shows. Dozens of productions (including some by Petipa), were brought out in accordance with the above-mentioned trends. They indeed might be listed under Imperial traditions. Of course I do not have in mind the best and most artistic creations of Petipa, connected with the Tchaikovsky reform or Glasunov's music.

When after the Revolution of 1917 the theatres were filled with new audiences representing the widest strata of society—workers, peasants, soldiers, and office employees, the question naturally arose what attitude to adopt towards an art, existing until then on the Imperial stage. Should it be cast away as something belonging altogether to the old world, or was it in need of reform?

For several years the doors of the theatres were open to the public free of charge. People were shown the ballets of the past: both the best of our classical heritage and ballets of the type mentioned above.

The new spectators passed their own judgement. Unconditionally they favoured the best ballets of the classical legacy. The most brilliant execution of such Petipa ballets as *La Fille du Pharaon*, *The Talisman*, *Le Roi Candaule* and so forth left them completely indifferent. At the same time they came to love not only *Swan Lake*, *The Sleeping Beauty* and *Giselle*, but also *La Fille Mal Gardée*, *Esmeralda* and *Don Quixote*, and this in spite of the fact that the form of expression was often quite old-fashioned, the productions outdated and the heroes themselves—fairies, princes, magicians and kings—completely alien to them.

Was this conservatism, was it backwardness? No, not at all! We ourselves did not quite understand at first that by making this selection the audiences were taking a healthy point of view on the culture of the past.

The culture of capitalist countries, Marx-Lenin aesthetics affirms, is not monolithic. Every capitalist country has two cultures; thus, we may say, in America there are two Americas, in France—two Frances, and in tsarist Russia there were two Russias. And there were two Russias in Russian art. One of them pandered to the tastes and needs of the patrons of the Imperial theatres. The other reflected the interests and tastes of broad democratic circles. In literature Pushkin and Gogol, Lermontov and Tolstoi, Chekhov and Gorky represented this democratic culture and were the true upholders of the interests of the people. And in music their counterparts were Glinka and Rimsky-Korsakov, Mussorgsky and Tchaikovsky.

Views on art, reflecting two different types of culture, also existed alongside one another in the Imperial ballet, at times blending into an alloy in a bizarre fashion. "Anti-Imperial" views upon ballet could not, quite naturally, prevail in an art dependent on the Imperial household. But they

111. Scene from the ballet *Laurencia*
112. Scene from the ballet *The Path of Thunder*

111

112

THE BRONZE HORSEMAN

113. Nina Chistova and Gennady Ledyakh as Parasha and Yevgeny
114. Peter the Great gives a ball (Alexander Radunsky as Peter the Great, Tamara Vetrova as Queen of the ball)
115. Tatyana Popko and Georgi Farmanyants as Columbina and Harlequin

114

115

CINDERELLA
116. Ball scene
117. Raisa Struchkova as Cinderella
118. Marina Kondratyeva as Cinderella

ROMEO AND JULIET
119. Galina Ulanova and Yuri Zhdanov
120. Galina Ulanova
121. Ball scene
122. Galina Ulanova and Yuri Zhdanov
123. Yaroslav Sekh as Mercutio
124. Duel scene (Alexei Yermolayev and
     Yuri Zhdanov as Tybalt and Romeo)

122

123

125

126

THE TALE OF THE STONE FLOWER

125. Dance of Semiprecious Stones
126. Maya Plisetskaya and Vladimir Levashov as the Mistress of
the Copper Mountain and Severyan
127. Vladimir Levashov as Severyan
128. Nina Timofeyeva as the Mistress of the Copper Mountain
129. Vladimir Vasilyev as Danila
130. Yekaterina Maximova and Vladimir Vasilyev as Katerina
and Danila

127

128

129

130

131

132

SPARTACUS

131. Scene from act 2 with Tamara Varlamova in the centre
132. Maya Plisetskaya and Nikolai Fadeyechev as Aegina and Harmodius
133. Prologue
134. Gladiators fighting
135. The dancing girls (Natalya Kasatkina and Ulameh Scott)

136

137

138

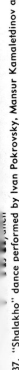

137. "Shalakho" dance performed by Ivan Pokrovsky, Mansur Kamaletdinov and Vladimir Vasilyev
138. Dance with tambourines
139. Mariam's dance (Nina Chkalova)
140. Raisa Struchkova and Yuri Kondratov as Gayaneh and Armen

141

142

143

144

145

PAGANINI
141-145. Yaroslav Sekh and Marina Kondratyeva as Paganini and the Muse

THE LITTLE HUMPBACKED HORSE

146-149. Scenes from the ballet (Vladimir Vasilyev as Ivanushka, Alexander Radunsky as the Tsar, Alla Shcherbinina as the Little Humpbacked Horse)

150. Alla Shcherbinina as the Little Humpbacked Horse

151. The final scene of the ballet. Yaroslav Sekh as Ivanushka and Rimma Karelskaya as Tsar-Maiden

"WALPURGIS NIGHT" (SCENE FROM CH. GOUNOD'S OPERA *FAUST*)

152. Bacchante (Olga Lepeshinskaya) and three satyrs
153. Three nymphs
154. Fragment from the ballet
155. Shamil Yagudin as faun
156. Bacchus (Vladimir Preobrazhensky) and three nymphs

found expression—sometimes more and sometimes less obviously—almost everywhere, practically in all noteworthy productions. All that has ever been produced for the entertainment of an empty-headed crowd is obsolete in our new ballet and should be discarded and forgotten. Such is the judgement prompted by experience. Soviet spectators have helped us to arrive at this judgement by demanding a critical approach to what we have inherited.

It became obvious that the calling of ballet, as of all arts, was to help the spectator to better understand himself and the world about him, to enrich his spiritual wealth and shape his ethical notions. Together with literature, drama and opera, ballet is a vehicle of education.

It goes without saying that variety of genres, types or forms is legitimate and welcome in ballet. There was a time when we rarely resorted to choreographic rendering of scores that had not been composed for ballet. We seldom used dance suites and almost completely ignored non-programmatic symphonies. We feared that choreography might become secondary to the music, while "danced music" might fail to convey the composer's conception and remain purely illustrative.

A demonstration of nothing but the beauty of form on the stage, however original such a work might be, is not good theatre. Theatre exists for the purpose of bringing out a living Man, whose thoughts, feelings and actions are motivated by life's vital problems. That is why theatres that lose interest in human spirit lose public recognition and the very right to bear the name of Theatre. As Stanislavsky used to say to young actors of the Bolshoi theatre, "they go in for purely external buffoonery and mannerisms: they try doing away with the curtain, next they place their settings upside down, or busy themselves with seeking a false rhythm of action, forgetting the one and only important thing—the human soul."

Noverre demanded less fairy-tales, less marvels and more scenes from real life. Dauberval said: "It is not enough for me to please the eye. I want to win the hearts." The masters of Soviet ballet believe they are the lawful heirs of the great men of choreographic thought because they are true to their forebears' most cherished principles. Let us remember the words of Mikhail Fokine: "However distant, however unrealistic does the art of dancing appear at first glance, it should contain its own truth of life if it is ever to have any value." How often people swear by the name of Fokine forgetting his principal canon!

Truly beautiful musical and choreographic creations boldly raise urgent problems of human existence, they always carry a message, ennobling and purifying. That is what gives them the right to immortality. Anything that fails to reach the public's mind and heart, that merely pleases the eye for a short moment, is doomed to early oblivion. These are not our words: they belong to the great Didelot. And here is the proof that he was right.

Dauberval's *La Fille Mal Gardée* is still popular and has been popular for over a century and a half. In spite of the naive and old-fashioned story, the theme of the ballet is dear to young generations of all epochs and nations. *Le Page Inconstant* was very soon forgotten, though here Dauberval displayed no less talent than in his other ballets, while the subject was borrowed from Beaumarchais' *Le Mariage de Figaro*. This happened because Dauberval used nothing but the *qui pro quo* from the comedy's one "mad day". The accusatory purpose of the comedy, directed against evil and bigotry, in other words its main idea, was practically left out.

Filippo Taglioni's *La Fille du Danube* to Adam's melodious music was deprived of a moving theme and soon went into oblivion, while his *La Sylphide*, so full of lyrical meditations that reflect the French Romanticism of the eighteen thirties is still alive.

116

Perrot's ballets *La Esmeralda, Ondine, Catarina,* born by an eager reaction to the popular thoughts and aspirations of his time, moved the hearts of generations of spectators, while such ballets as *Armide, La Filleule des Fées* and *Éoline ou la Dryade* faded before they blossomed, though Perrot's brilliance as choreographer was as high in these as in any other of his ballets.

For us there are not only two of Petipa, but also two of Fokine. One of these we admire. The attitude to the other is negative. This verdict has been also pronounced by the spectators. It gives the reason perhaps why some of the Fokine ballets (among them *Les Sylphides, Polovtsian Dances,* and *The Dying Swan*) never leave the stage, while some of his other brilliant tableaux (for instance, *Schéhérazade*) are almost forgotten.

Apparently dance form alone, however original, does not make for lasting and true popularity if it lacks depth of meaning and thought.

Hardly a dozen ballets have survived from among the thousands created since the days of Noverre. Time has mercilessly rejected all those "hits" of the day, once amazing their contemporaries by their motley splendour and novelty of form. Only the truly precious and beautiful creations have been spared.

A striving to reflect the inner substance of life has become part and parcel of Soviet choreography. Soviet art cannot isolate itself from its people. This is what constitutes its novelty of principle, its entirely new mission.

It is hardly necessary to emphasise that this alone makes Soviet ballet radically different to the Imperial theatre. In those days ballet kept to the side of the road taken by literature and other arts, coming in contact with them only occasionally, whereas now it takes part in the assertion of our artistic ideals openly and directly as an equal of other arts.

Progressive art was always drawn to great literature. Literature is a wise mother that can endow its offsprings with a wealth of ideas and imagery. Its ability to penetrate beyond the surface of life cannot be equalled. Soviet ballet sees a life-giving source for further development in joining forces with literature—both classical and contemporary.

Turning to Pushkin, Lermontov, Shakespeare, Balzac, Lope de Vega, Gogol, Goldoni, N. Ostrovsky, Bazhov and other classical and modern writers, Soviet choreographers and producers borrowed from them lofty ideas, a depth of content and poetic imagery, and sought to clothe them in a new choreographic form.

Soviet libretto authors have a fascinating task ahead. With the successful experience of basing their work on classical literature to fall back on, they have to create books of ballets depicting the heroism, greatness and romance of our today.

The best choreographers of the past used to dream of a union of author, musician, choreographer and designer. However, in Soviet ballet alone this alliance became a necessity and therefore a law. It is immaterial by whom the book is conceived—by the choreographer, composer or professional writer. What matters is that the dramaturgical outline of the production is sketched long before the composer conceives the first bar of the music and the choreographer—the first step of the ballet. This outline is not a framework on which music and dance are simply stretched. It finds expression in terms of musical and dance imagery. The general underlying idea of the story and, therefore, of the future production, is of primary importance in Soviet ballet. The substance of this idea is embedded in the book. And this also makes Soviet ballet an antipode of the Imperial ballet.

Literature and art of every epoch have their own positive heroes. The history of ballet is also characterised by the search for a positive hero as a medium for expressing the author's attitude to reality.

Take, for instance, the children of "the third estate" of the French revolution—Lise and Colas from Dauberval's *La Fille Mal Gardée*. Or take the heroes of the French romantic ballets of the 1830s and the 1840s. They refuse to reconcile themselves with the world of cheap virtue and the cynical worship of money, and die in unequal struggle with their milieu.

The squalor of life made the author of romantic ballets turn to fantasy. In the world of dreams it was easier to counterpose an imaginary hero to a "hero" borrowed from life that was not worthy of extolling.

The fate of the heroine in *Giselle* was the fate of many in the France of the 1830s. Giselle is the blood-sister of Coralie in Balzac's *Les Illusions Perdues* or of the heroes of Berlioz's *Symphonie Fantastique*. Different artists had different solutions for the problems agitating their minds. "Paris is a den of talents, a prison of minds, where faith in the fine things disappears and the fine things themselves perish." These words of Balzac are given a poetic scenic life in *Giselle*.

The search for a new hero, started by West-European ballet in mid-19th century was continued by Russian ballet. Struggle for human dignity constituted the *leitmotif* of the best Russian productions in the second half of the last century. Honour is worth fighting and dying for—such is the conclusion reached by the heroes of the Tchaikovsky ballets. In his works there is no contrasting of the hero to the crowd, as there is in the romantic French ballets of the 19th century (for instance, in *La Esmeralda*).

The absence of heroes in capitalist society has become an almost insurmountable obstacle on the path of choreographic development. Many French, British and American ballets of today simply do without a hero.* The characters of such ballets are deprived of moral ideals since the authors cannot find any in the morals of the ruling classes.

It is well known, however, that in works of art ethics is inseparable from aesthetics. Only that is beautiful which is beautiful in thought, feeling and deed. Such is the secret of true poetry.

In championing these principles, Soviet ballet breaks with the so-called "Imperial traditions" of Russian ballet in this respect as well. The Revolution gave birth to poetry all about us, on the earth that is being transformed with our own hands, and there was no need any more to look for it in the realm of beautiful fantasy. Poetry, truth, beauty is to be found not in exaggerated praise of the past, in romantic illusions, or in escape from reality, but in fighting for its ideals. Life offers us prototypes of a positive hero at every step. He is the rank-and-file but in no way run-of-the-mill toiler, he is the creator of mankind's new history. In 1919, Maxim Gorky was dreaming of a "hero nobly self-forgetting, passionately in love with his ideal, a hero in the true, broad sense of the word".

The hero of Soviet ballet is moved by love for humanity and an infinite faith in man's moral strength, he is moved by hatred of anything that prevents a full flowering of spiritual forces, that stifles man and takes away his right to peaceful labour and personal happiness.

Our theatre asserts an inseparable bond between social and private destiny and interests. For the first time the theme of the Revolution took possession of the ballet stage. The dancers were faced with a new task: more passion and energy had to be introduced into their acting. Events of

* See the article "The Legendary Hero" by Alexander Bland in the *Ballet Annual* No. 15

popular life lent an atmosphere of heroism and pathos to the productions. The People as the leading hero came to the foreground.

Any theme—be it fairy-tale, or historical, has to be interpreted with a contemporary vision. Otherwise there will be no authenticity, no artistic merit, no chance of "immortality" for that work of art.

The powerful current of life brought new heroes to the Soviet ballet, such as had not been known for too long a time. These heroes are compatriots and contemporaries of the spectators. No matter how much we criticised these new characters sometimes, they did invariably introduce something *new* into art—they endowed the heroes with great generosity, with a feeling of solidarity and fraternity, with a burning concern for the fate of the people in all the parts of the world.

Our spectator always sides with those fighting for a just cause. He shows lively interest in events taking place in any part of the universe at any period.

Before the Revolution, the world that came into the ballet's line of vision was restricted to five or six countries. Today it is the whole globe. Ancient Rome, old Georgia, Spain of Renaissance, medieval Azerbaijan and the contemporary times ranging from South Africa to the Soviet Union—the action of Soviet ballets takes place in all of these, dancing love and hatred, challenge to death and glorification of life.

To tackle the new themes, create new characters, and become one of the branches of "the science of man", Soviet ballet had to find its own ways of cognizing and portraying reality in art. The search for these new methods was prolonged and complicated and is still going on. We have tried out the whole range of existing means, and we can say with complete assurance that impressionism, expressionism, urbanism, constructivism, symbolism and abstract art are powerless to pose the vital problems of life or to penetrate the inner depths of human soul. Sooner or later progressive artists the world over will become convinced of this through personal experience.

The method of socialist realism, which is the method of Soviet art, took form gradually. Life has proved that it enables us better than any other method to depict themes from reality and to create psychologically complex and truthful characters of contemporary heroes. Realism is in no way a monopoly of Soviet ballet. It is accessible to any artist of the dance, who looks for beauty in life and for a way to the hearts of his audience.

Many foreign critics do not discriminate between two trends in art—realism and naturalism. Naturalism, in actual fact, is a bitter enemy of realism. Whereas realism selects from life that which is most important, what moves man and humanity, naturalism shows up everything that falls within its vision and so turns art into something worse than a photograph—a dreary, dull record registering facts, but incapable of conveying their inner significance. Realism catches the very heartbeat of the times. It penetrates the very core of human existence and discovers its hidden springs. It generalises events, revealing the general through the particular, finding something essential for all and for everyone in separately taken phenomena.

A blind copying of nature is a sister of naturalistic illustration. Stage episodes then serve the sole purpose of illustrating the author's idea; but they do not light it from within with the author's peculiar *vision*. This deprives the ballet of ideological and artistic impact. Soviet theatre is ceaselessly struggling against the method of illustration, which is inimical to realism.

Truth of emotions, truth of character should be reproduced in close contact with reality, in accordance with the driving forces of a definite period in the life of a people, a country, or of humanity as a whole.

Let us quote just one example. In Soviet ballet there are many so-called "eternal themes". Among them is the theme of tragic love, thwarted by insurmountable obstacles set by society. Alongside with the Shakespeare ballet about the star-crossed lovers of Verona at least two more have emerged. These are *Leili and Mejnun* to music by Balasanyan, and *The Path of Thunder* to music by Karayev.

What is it that distinguishes Leili and Mejnun from Romeo and Juliet or Sarie and Lanny? Details of their love? The circumstances? Difference of folklore or place of action? Separate episodes? Characters of the opponents to their love? No. The eternal and seemingly parallel theme is given different shape by life itself. The destiny of forbidden love in the era of Arabian and Central Asian Middle Ages is radically different from that of forbidden love on the eve of European Renaissance. And forbidden love of a coloured man for a white girl in the Union of South Africa of our day has its own peculiar features, introduced by contemporaneity.

Leili and Mejnun's love had its own historically determined limitations. The significance of their love lies in non-acceptance of age-old laws. The passionate lovers had neither the strength nor the courage to fight for their happiness. Their belated reunion came to them only on their deathbed.

Romeo and Juliet's love had an entirely different scope. Leili and Mejnun's suffering in solitude is replaced by happiness of fulfilment. Instead of the protest against living "in the old way" comes a desire to "live in a new way", and the latter desire triumphs, even though the lovers pay with their lives for it.

Sarie and Lanny—heroes of Peter Abrahams' novel and of Karayev's ballet—knew the happiness of love without hiding in the shadow of the night, as did Romeo and Juliet. Sarie and Lanny defend their happiness with arms in hand. A way out, albeit a tragic one, has now been found for a situation which appeared hopeless in many works dedicated to forbidden love. Struggle for life to the last breath comes now to replace death as the inevitable outcome of forbidden love and the only possible union of lovers.

Time has not only determined the extent to which feeling has been emancipated, but also the attitude of the surrounding society towards the lovers.

Only an art that has acquired depth of thought and scope of observation is capable of such penetration. Broad horizons of life have been opened for Soviet ballet.

Fairy-tales and legends used to prevail in ballet. These themes appear in Soviet ballets alongside of those borrowed from real life. The method of realism, enabling us to extract poetry out of the "prose" of reality, also made it possible to portray the characters of ordinary flesh-and-blood people through the dance idiom.

In the course of at least a century, ballet revolved round the theme of romantic love. Now *any* great love—love for one's family, friends, children, work, creations, motherland—all this becomes part of ballet. Therefore the very scope of this art has become considerably expanded.

In pre-revolutionary ballets the characters, as a rule, were static. They did not change as the plot developed. Realism armed Soviet ballet with a versatility of characters, such as had been characteristic of drama or opera. From the beginning to the end of the performance the character grows and develops: struggle makes his love nobler and purer and his hatred stronger; new feelings, new attitudes are born in him. Thus grows the tension of passions and the tension of ideas, clashing in conflict.

Realism has made *life in dance* an absolute law of scenic behaviour. The dancer lives, breathes, thinks—all in terms of dance. That is why the dramatic narrative in a ballet is not counterposed to dance. One follows from the other, forming a single whole.

Realism in Soviet art is essentially different from realism of the past century. Let us take, for instance, its relations with romanticism. Our realism is not an antipode of romanticism, as it was in the last century. In order to sing the ideals of contemporaneity our realism uses methods of inspired romanticism. Realities of life are given a romantic form. In other words our realism is inseparable from revolutionary romanticism. Our ballet uses more and more often the theme of romantic heroic deeds in the name of humanity's ideals, in the exploration of new planets, in making new scientific discoveries. This is a romanticism of emotions, freed from prejudices of a society divided into classes and torn by contradictions.

Socialist realism does not tolerate ready-made formulas. Choreographers must demonstrate a variety of style, method and personal touches. Soviet ballet uses both the highly metaphorical poetical imagery and "simple talk"—i.e., narrative, which seems at first glance ordinary and commonplace.

Ballets-*divertissements*, choreographic comedies and dramas, dance poems—any type of spectacle is desirable for Soviet ballet. It leans, however, in the direction of large canvases. Let us be quite frank—it is much more difficult to create these than one-act miniatures. Nevertheless, Soviet choreographers are also interested in genre tableaux, in sketches and small choreographic compositions.

Least of all the predilection for full-length dance narrative is explained by clinging to traditions: huge monoliths of ballets in the Imperial theatres were usually nothing but slightly disguised *divertissements*, a kind of choreographic *revue* or *féerie*, while in Soviet ballet we are dealing with large-scale symphonic canvases wherein the action develops at a great dramatic tension.

Involved musical drama requires not just narrative episodes but, also, and mainly, episodes in which the facts narrated are emotionally explained. Imagine a piece of music consisting of nothing but themes, shorn of any further development!

The amorous dialogues of Odette and Siegfried need the accompaniment of the swans' dances. The destiny of Albrecht and Giselle is supported by dances of the Wilis. But even these (e. g., dance of the four cygnets and so forth) are not infrequently classed as pure *divertissement*, in other words an interpolated and disposable body.

Some of our Soviet ballets suffer from an over-abundance of detail, that swells the action out of all proportion; quite a few things could be cut without any harm. But these isolated criticisms do not infringe in any way on the principles of Soviet ballet.

We wish to live through the development of the poetic plot together with the authors and the dancers. Step by step we want to take part in their struggle for the ideal, to share with them the joy of victory or the sorrow of defeat. When the heroes' destiny is linked with that of his nation, his story can't be reduced to so many short episodes. The art of *performance* (such was the Imperial ballet) becomes an art of *living the role*. The psychological development of characters and situations which, as a rule, was absent in the old days, becomes a necessity in every production.

Some theorists and practicians of ballet in the West draw a line between tradition and innovation in art. But in reality tradition and innovation are not antagonistic. They are two facets of one and the same process, quite inseparable from one another. Innovation does not mean breaking with traditions or replacing the one with the other through suppression and destruction; it means a development of traditions through reform, effected *from within*. Traditions are strong because they

157

158

159

160

161

162

163

157-163. Galina Ulanova coaches
Yekaterina Maximova
for Giselle

survive their own time and serve the new time—while being at the same time transformed by it. A genuine revolution in ballet is invariably the fruit of daring creative evolution.

Before creating the new, the old—that is of the legacy of the past—has to be fully mastered. Experience of both pre-revolutionary and Soviet ballet has taught us this lesson, which will sooner or later be learned by ballet in every other country as well. There is no art in which devotion to traditions is of such paramount importance as in ballet.

At least two national ballets—the French and the Russian—toiled for over three quarters of a century to make *Giselle* immortal. The beginnings of *Giselle* may be traced in the ballets *Cupid and Psyche* by Dauberval, Noverre and Didelot, Dauberval's *La Fille Mal Gardée*, Milon's *Nina ou la Folle par Amour*, Didelot's *Flore et Zéphyre*, Aumer's *La Somnambule*, Filippo Taglioni's *La Sylphide*, *La Fille du Danube*, and, more directly, *L'Écumeur de Mer*, not to mention many other sources. The *Giselle* of 1841 could not have come into existence without these, just as the *Giselle* of 1960 would not have been what it is without Perrot's *Ondine*, Petipa's *La Bayadere* and *The Sleeping Beauty* and Lev Ivanov's scenes from *Swan Lake*.

It is indisputable that Fokine was an innovator. However, the new in his work grew out of the experience of his predecessors and contemporaries. The butt of Fokine's attacks was directed against the "old ballet" of Petipa and others, and yet this very "old" ballet helped him in shaping the "new". His *Dying Swan* would never have been born without *Swan Lake*, his *Cléopâtre*—without *La Fille du Pharaon* in Gorsky's revised version, and his *Le Carnaval* would never have come into existence without Petipa's *Les Millions d'Arlequin*. Fokine's use of symphonic music for dance was preceded by fruitful work in the same direction done first by Petipa and Ivanov, and later by Gorsky.

At one time, attempts were made to tie down the system of the classical dance to a definite country or a definite class, and to treat it as a product of that given epoch. It was declared that it was as changeable as the times and styles that had engendered it, and should therefore be replaced by something else.

The past few decades have proved the fallacy of such views.

Classical dancing is the quintessence of artistically generalised human movements. It is immortal when regarded as a foundation on which choreographers, musicians, ballerinas and *danseurs* build their images. Without the classical dance as the artistic language of ballet, there is no ballet. True, once the classical dance is regarded as a set of pretty gestures and steps, it loses its meaning. The use of conventional school exercises for any situation and any image inevitably leads to formalism and naturalism. Even the most cunning pattern-creating pleasing for the moment is sterile and doomed to oblivion if it is conceived outside of content.

Contrarywise, the deeper the choreographer's perception of life, the more eloquent becomes the classical dance idiom of the characters created by his inspiration.

There are no limits to the flexibility of the classical dance, provided the choreographers know how to use it. Classical dance should, indeed, be enriched and modernised—but according to its laws and purpose (that of creating an image), rather than the choreographers' whims. Classical dancing, more readily than any other kind, blends with the music, comprising a "choreographic melody". If the very nature of classical dancing is ignored, this "melody" disappears, beauty goes too, and the ugly and deformed takes possession of the stage.

However, content must be given priority if art is to attain the maximum of expression. New content is what suggests and engenders new form. New form in itself can never give birth to corresponding content. Form-making is always sterile.

The system of classical dance is an evergreen tree of scenic expression. Anything may be grafted to it. Taking this system as a basis, the choreographer should enrich and expand it. Folk dances, grotesque, acrobatics, ballroom dancing, eurythmics—all this should be made into a new alloy by force of the choreographer's imagination, an alloy best suited to the images he has in mind. It is of paramount importance to remember that stage dancing has several aspects, and the preference of one to the detriment of the rest invariably ends in disaster. Only a blend of technical virtuosity, plastic expressiveness and poetic content is capable of sustaining realism in ballet.

In ballets based on new material taken directly from life the expressiveness of dance form sometimes falls short of the content. Though quite logical at the beginning, this cannot be long tolerated. Not all Soviet choreographers display enough daring and inventiveness in their use of accepted ballet forms. However, our faith in the chosen means and methods is none the weaker for it. They are correct—therefore the imperfections will be overcome.

Folklore has blossomed in Soviet society. Dozens and hundreds of folk dances of diverse nationalities have become widely popular. This has a fruitful influence on ballet.

In Imperial ballet national dances were used mostly in *divertissements*. Gorsky and Fokine were the first to make an attempt at creating the character through folk dance steps. Take the Archer in *Polovtsian Dances* and the characters in *Jota Aragonesa*. Soviet ballet has gone much further. Elements of folk and classical dancing are blended so harmoniously in its dance portrayals, that often it is difficult to tell which of the colours have been used in painting the portrait. Folk dancing lends national colour and authenticity to the characters, it opens up new horizons for the development of the art of dancing, offering as it does a wealth of new and original styles of choreography.

Soviet choreographers often resort to methods of plastic recitative borrowed from different forms of pantomime. The best creations of our choreographers are based on a union of dance and mime.

The tremendous importance of music must also be noted. Soviet choreographers do not share the point of view, widespread abroad, that music is self-sufficient or merely auxiliary. Prokofiev, Khachaturyan and Karayev imbue their ballet music with a wealth of emotion, dramatic tension and poetic content. Music like that is a real friend of the dance.

* * *

The Orphanage building still faces the Moskva River and the Kremlin. But there are no longer any orphans there, nor does it train dancers any more.

Now there is more than one ballet stage in the capital. The majestic Bolshoi Theatre stands in a beautiful square. Its ballet school is near by. In 1961, the building of the Palace of Congresses in the Kremlin grounds with a hall seating 6,000 was completed. Here, the ballet of the Bolshoi Theatre gives regular performances of *Swan Lake*, *Nutcracker* and *The Fountain of Bakhchisarai*. In Pushkin street is the Stanislavsky and Nemirovich-Danchenko Musical Theatre with its repertoire of original ballets.

The ballet company of the Bolshoi has more than 200 members and a reserve of more than 350 pupils. The Bolshoi Ballet School gives recitals and stages ballets that are very popular.

164. On the stage
165-169. . . . and behind the scenes

170. Conductor Yuri Fayer
171. Balletmaster Leonid Lavrovsky with young dancers

165

168

166

169

167

The Bolshoi stage is 26 metres deep. It takes a huge company to fill a stage of such dimensions. That is why the Bolshoi permanently employs 75 supers, forming the so-called "mime ensemble", well trained in the rudiments of dancing and acting.

Last but not least we must mention another participant in these shows: the spectator, who is the most active and enthusiastic participant of all. The Bolshoi rings with applause as Prince Siegfried conquers the Evil Magician, as Mercutio does a merry dance to draw Tybalt's attention away from Romeo, as Juliet, wrapped in a cape, runs along the streets of Verona, as if hurrying to give battle for her love, or as the Mistress of the Copper Mountain punishes the villainous Severyan. With this applause the spectators show their sympathy for the hero and side with all those who fight for the rightful cause, for man's happiness.

Soviet society has not only prepared ballet for the spectator, but the spectator for ballet. Over a million adults study dancing in various amateur theatrical groups. Several million children are taught elements of ballet dancing along with singing and music. These people watch ballet productions with a keen professional eye that is exacting but friendly. It is not a handful of "abonnées" or the "chosen public" that are interested in the art of dancing, it is the whole people.

172. Balletmaster Rostislav Zakharov with the composer Reinhold Glière and libret Pyotr Abolimov at a rehearsal of his ballet The Bronze Horseman
173. Balletmaster Vasily Vainonen at the première of his ballet Nutcracker

BALLETS CHOREOGRAPHED AFTER SCENARIOS
BY YURI SLONIMSKY

Ballet	Composer	Choreographer	Theatre	Date	Designer
Christmas Eve	B. Asafiev	V. Varkovitsky	Ballet School, Leningrad	15/VI 1938	A. Kolomoitsev
Christmas Eve	B. Asafiev	F. Lopukhov	Art Theatre of Ballet headed by V. Krieger, Moscow	29/XII 1938	B. Knoblok
Nightingale	M. Kroshner	A. Yermolayev	Minsk Opera and Ballet Theatre	7/XI 1939	B. Matrunin
Tale of a Priest and his Hired Man Balda	M. Chulaki	V. Varkovitsky	Maly Opera Theatre, Leningrad	9/I 1940	A. Kolomoitsev
Spring Fairy-Tale	B. Asafiev after music by P. Tchaikovsky	F. Lopukhov	Kirov Opera and Ballet Theatre, Leningrad	8/I 1947	S. Virsaladze
Youth	M. Chulaki	B. Fenster	Maly Opera Theatre, Leningrad	9/XII 1949	T. Bruni
Seven Beauties	Kara Karayev	P. Gusev	Akhundov Opera and Ballet Theatre, Baku	6/XI 1952	E. Almaszade and N. Gusak
The Path of Thunder	Kara Karayev	K. Sergeyev	Kirov Opera and Ballet Theatre, Leningrad	31/XII 1957	V. Dorer
Coast of Hope	Andrei Petrov	I. Belsky	Kirov Opera and Ballet Theatre, Leningrad	16/VI 1959	V. Dorer

YURI SLONIMSKY'S WORKS

1. *Giselle*. Leningrad, 1926 (monograph).

2. *La Sylphide*. Leningrad, 1927 (monograph).

3. *Masters of the Ballet of the 19th Century*. Leningrad, 1937.

4. *Classics of Choreography*. Leningrad, 1937. Publication of the Leningrad State Choreographic school. Introductory articles: "Choreography of Carlo Blasis" and "Balletmaster Bournonville".

5. "Birth of the Moscow Ballet". Introductory article in: A. Gluszkowski. *Reminiscences of a Balletmaster*, Moscow, 1940. Publication of the Bolshoi Theatre Ballet School.

6. "Progress of Character Dancing". Introductory article in the book: *Fundamentals of Character Dancing* by A. Lopukhov, A. Shirayev, A. Bocharov. Publication of the Leningrad State Choreographic School, Leningrad, 1939.

7. "Theatrical Paris of the Eighteen Thirties". Introductory article in the souvenir programme: *Lost Illusions* issued in connection with the first production of that ballet, Leningrad, 1936.

8. "At the Cradle of the Russian Terpsichore". Introductory article to I. Valberg's book *From the Balletmaster's Archives* and editing of diaries, correspondence and scenarios for ballets, comprising this volume. Moscow, 1948.

9. *Soviet Ballet*. Articles in the book *Soviet Ballet*, Yuri Slonimsky, editor, New York, *Philosophical Library*, 1947.

10. *Soviet Ballet*. Iskustvo, Moscow-Leningrad, 1950. (Contains a full list of Soviet ballets with dates of first performances.)

11. *Tchaikovsky and the Ballet Theatre of His Time*. Moscow, Music Publishing House, 1956.

12. *The Bolshoi Theatre Ballet*. Foreign Languages Publishing House, Moscow, 1956.

13. *Ballet Annual No. 12*, London, 1957. "In Pursuit of the New". Article.

14. *Didelot*. Landmarks of his creative biography. Leningrad, 1958.

15. *Ballet Annual No. 13*, London, 1958. "A Letter on Soviet Ballet". Article.

16. *Ballet Annual No. 14*, London, 1959. "Soviet Ballet, 1958-59. The Problem of Reviving the Classics and of Producing Works with a Contemporary Theme". Article.

17. *Ballet Annual No. 15*, 1960. "Cradle of the Russian Ballet: the History of the Leningrad Ballet Company". Article.

Also numerous articles and ballet reviews in Soviet periodicals.

Printed in the Union of Soviet Socialist Republics